BEST OF
JOE BONAMASSA

Contents

This book was approved by Joe Bonamassa

Cover photos by Koerhsen & Marty Richards

Transcribed by Andrew Moore and Paul Pappas

Cherry Lane Music Company
Director of Publications/Project Editor: Mark Phillips
Manager of Publications: Gabrielle Fastman

ISBN-13: 978-1-57560-894-5
ISBN-10: 1-57560-894-4

Visit our website at www.cherrylane.com

Joe Bonamassa

"I'm the luckiest guy in the world," said virtuoso blues-rock guitarist, singer-songwriter, and Blues Foundation board member and spokesperson Joe Bonamassa. For a young artist who's living his dream, it's an apt summation of the story so far. Bonamassa's latest album, *You & Me*, debuted at #1 on *Billboard* magazine's Blues chart in June 2006. All his previous albums have either hit #1 or gone Top 10 on that same chart. He plays well over 150 dates a year in the U.S. and internationally—a touring legacy that began when the legendary B.B. King invited Joe, at age 12, to come on the road with him as his opening act. He is the youngest member of the 25-person national Board of Directors for the Memphis-based Blues Foundation, and is the leading advocate for their acclaimed Blues in the Schools program.

Much about how Bonamassa achieved so much so early is familiar lore by now. At age four he played a short-scale Chiquita guitar given to him by his father, a guitar dealer and player himself. "I always want to remember," Joe says, "taking to guitar like a duck takes to water." By the time he was seven, he had stepped up to a full-scale model and was burning up Stevie Ray Vaughan licks. At ten, Joe was gigging at venues in upstate New York, near his hometown of Utica, and that's how he came to B.B. King's attention. After initially hearing Bonamassa play, the blues icon—who personally asked Joe to open for his landmark 2005 80th Birthday Celebration Tour—said, "This kid's potential is unbelievable. He hasn't even begun to scratch the surface. He's one of a kind."

When King first took the "kid" on tour, it was an invaluable education for Joe. Soon, Bonamassa had also sat in with Buddy Guy and John Lee Hooker and had opened for many other acts, including Foreigner, George Thorogood, Peter Frampton, Robert Cray, Danny Gatton, Stephen Stills, Joe Cocker, and Gregg Allman. Repeatedly, artists that Joe played with became fans of his as well, and he continues to work with most of them, ever building on his reputation as a consummate player. Venerable producer Phil Ramone once said of Joe, "prodigies come few and far between. I saw him take an audience apart." Accepted by old-guard masters and his peers alike, Bonamassa has an audience of fans as generation-spanning as his famed collaborators.

Joe's recording career began in the very early '90s, after he met Berry Oakley Jr., son of the Allman Brothers Band bassist. They put together Bloodline, a group also featuring Robby Krieger's son Waylon and Miles Davis's son Erin. The band released an acclaimed self-titled album and won praise for their hard-charging fusion of blues, funk, boogie, and roadhouse rock. Touring with Bloodline further seasoned Bonamassa's performance skills and made it clear to audiences everywhere that while he obviously channeled traditional, swampy blues with the best of them, he rocked equally hard. The blues was a foundation rather than a final destination, and Joe is as much a dynamic bridge to its future as a living link to its past.

The full range of Bonamassa's talents came into sharper relief after Bloodline disbanded. Organically fusing rock 'n' roll influences and contemporary sensibilities with the blues, Joe's solo music is a rich modern hybrid all its own—one that has also heralded Bonamassa's emergence as a powerful singer. "That was a new direction I felt I had to pursue when I set out on my own," says Joe. "I just started belting things out and I found this voice I never knew I had. Because I was untrained as a vocalist, there was nothing holding me back. I'd play around with emulating some of my favorite singers—Paul Rodgers, Gregg Allman, Rod Stewart. Sometimes it was frustrating. I'd been playing guitar for so long, and had gotten control over that, but this was uncharted territory. Ultimately, it's allowed me a freedom as an artist I hadn't felt before."

Joe's muscular fusion of righteous playing and keenly etched vocals has never been more seamless than on his latest solo album, You & Me. Produced by South African–born studio ace Kevin Shirley—whose credits include Led Zeppelin, the Black Crowes, Aerosmith, and Joe Satriani—the disc potently blends a "big rock sound," intense British blues (about which Joe's especially passionate), and gritty Delta roots. It's packed with standouts, including an interpretation of Charley Patton's "High Water Everywhere" (a tribute to New Orleans), "So Many Roads" (a blues classic made famous by Otis Rush), and "Tea for One," a Zeppelin gem embellished with a full orchestra—and Jason Bonham on drums. Bonamassa, who's been getting deeper into songwriting, also cites the originals "Bridge to Better Days" and the Ray Charles–inflected "Asking Around for You" as favorites.

You & Me is mature work that continues to unspool the artistic thread that began with Bonamassa's solo debut, 2000's Top 10 Blues disc A New Day Yesterday, named for the 1969 Jethro Tull classic that Joe makes his own with (as allmusic.com calls it) "a jaw-dropping performance." Produced by the legendary Tom Dowd—whose career included work with Aretha Franklin, Ornette Coleman, Eric Clapton, Ray Charles, John Coltrane, Rod Stewart, and scores of others—the album features guest shots by Gregg Allman, Rick Derringer, and Leslie West, among other greats. The powerhouse original song "Miss You, Hate You" remains a cornerstone of Joe's repertoire, as does the slide guitar showcase "Cradle Rock." In 2002 Bonamassa released So, It's Like That, a brew of dead-on blues and classic pop-rock production featuring all originals, including the tour de force "Pain and Sorrow." The album was his first to hit #1 on Billboard's Blues chart.

In 2003—designated "Year of the Blues" by Congress—Bonamassa returned with his heartfelt tribute to the genre, Blues Deluxe, packed with nine classics and three originals. In the liner notes, Harris Cohen observes that Joe "never loses touch with the raw emotion that makes the blues what it is." Reviewing Blues Deluxe, former Creem editor Jaan Uhelszki added, "New York guitar phenom walks tall in the blues tradition…jettisoning fiery riffs inspired by John Lee Hooker, B.B. King, Elmore James, and Albert Collins into the future with furious playing, a hard-rock sensibility, and a grizzled voice that owes a debt to Gregg Allman. Equally inspired by the Delta blues and the mid-'60s British blues boom, the young firebrand…is able to fuse those two schools together, creating edgy blues-rock." Bonamassa further honed that fusion on 2004's Had to Cry Today, another sweat-soaked mix of innovative and classic sounds made electrifying through his gale force playing.

Bonamassa is also deeply committed to Blues in the Schools, developed by the Memphis-based Blues Foundation to educate students about the legacy of the blues and to promote and preserve its heritage. Joe has helped bring the program into over 100 schools across the country, and response has prompted the Foundation to indefinitely extend it. "I love the way the kids' eyes light up," says Joe. "We introduce them to Muddy Waters, Robert Johnson, and other legends. I explain this amazing musical family tree to them, and talk about how almost every artist today can be traced back to the origins of blues and jazz." In 2005 Bonamassa became the youngest-ever member of the Blues Foundations' 25-person Board of Directors. "When they told me my name was in the hat for it," he remembers, "I had that 'it's nice just to be nominated' feeling. Then I was on a plane to Memphis to actually become a part of it, and it was an incredible honor."

Currently, when not performing shows as one of the hardest-working artists on the road today, Bonamassa is writing material for an acoustic album he's planning to release in 2007. "I'm known as an electric guitar player," he says, "but a big part of my music started on the acoustic end, and I want to also show that side of me." Born on May 8, 1977 (the day that would have been blues icon Robert Johnson's 66th birthday), Joe lives in Los Angeles with his ever-growing collection of vintage and custom-made guitars (now reaching the 200 mark). "I still feel like same four-year-old who just got his first guitar for Christmas," says Joe—with a passion that's heard in every note he plays.

Joe Bonamassa: The Interview
by John Stix

The book opens with "Blues Deluxe," a cover tune off one of my favorite albums, Jeff Beck's *Truth*. Why did you choose this particular song?

When I first heard it on *Truth*, I thought they covered this classic blues song. I realized it was by Rod Stewart. It was like an instant classic. They did it so heavy and it was great. I really enjoyed doing an interpretation of it and it took me a while to do this because I couldn't sing that high. I had to wait for my voice to catch up with my desire to do the song. We played it live as a band for probably two years before we recorded it. Then when we finally recorded it, we did two takes. The only thing we subsequently added was keyboards. The solo is live; I sang it live and everything was live. I think it's one of the coolest tracks I've ever recorded. It captures the band in the room as it was played. There wasn't a whole lot of thought process; there was no messing with the arrangement; there was no click track. It was just a natural band playing a song and being captured live. The version that we ended up using was the first take.

Everybody said, "Wow, we should at least try one more take to see." The second take wasn't as good, so we were like, "That's it; we're done."

You start with just touch and phrasing. You use volume swells and go pedal to the metal.

It was really instrumental for me not to just do the Gary Moore unabashed wailing. The cake is in the notes. There had to be a part of that, but I think I'm trying to make a definitive version. We could take this thing that Jeff Beck did and just put it on steroids. It's fast and easy to do that. But that doesn't take a whole lot of thought process. I was trying to make a different yet definitive version of that song.

I produced Al Pitrelli and halfway though the song I told him to drop his pick. It put him in a new place and would force him to think differently.

Yeah, that really is the bottom line, having maybe a little bit of a handicap. Maybe you don't use the pick—you try something different and you are put in a situation where you are not completely comfortable. But you can get really cool, creative things that come out of that.

I felt the soloing here reflected more your take on Albert King and Stevie Ray Vaughan.

I did it with a Strat. I now play it with a Les Paul. For me it took on a life of its own. It was definitely more my Albert King moment. It was me trying to do an amalgamation of Albert King and Jeff Beck.

Talk for a moment about playing with pick vs. playing with the fingers.

I go back and forth all the time between using pick and fingers. I never even think about it anymore. I use the pick for some fast notes and I use my fingers for some fast notes; it just depends on what I'm doing. I do like having the feel of going back and forth. You get a better tone when you play with your fingers. I think for chords it's even better.

Did you practice the volume swells?

I don't really practice them. The hard part of doing the volume swell is moving from a Strat to a Les Paul. With

the Les Paul you can't do it on the front pickup. You need a really bright tone and a good volume pot.

What's the difference between playing this song on a Strat and a Les Paul?

I think it sounds less like Stevie Ray. Anybody doing slow blues playing the fast stuff with the Strat is immediately in that category of being Stevie Ray Vaughan. I am a big fan of Stevie, but he was not my primary influence.

Almost every guitar stylist I've spoken with goes through what I call the imitation/innovation transformation. You start by imitating your favorite players, and at some point you evolve and innovate your own

style. **When did this first happen with you?**

I'm still working on it. I grew out of the "I want to be somebody else" phase around age 16. Before that I thought if I could just be a copy of Eric Johnson or Danny Gatton, that would be great. For me, the stage when I got out of that deal was when I realized I'm never going to be Eric Johnson. I'll never be as fast as Eric Johnson. I'm never going to be as well versed as Danny Gatton. I'm never going to have the tone or phrasing of Eric Clapton, so I might as well just do it myself.

When you were in the band Bloodline, were you still within the imitation phase?

It was mostly the imitation phase, because I was heavily into Stevie Ray and Robin Trower and those kinds of guys. After Bloodline, Tom Dowd was really instrumental in helping me find my own voice. When we recorded my first solo album, *A New Day Yesterday*, he would basically say, "Here is where you sound like Albert King, here is where you sound like Jeff Beck, here is where you sound like you." He worked with every guitar player and he goes, "Trust me, this is where you sound like an original guitar player." I went, "Oh!" That was really insightful because nobody had ever said that to me before. I had been called into these sessions and they would say we need something like a Jeff Beck thing or we need a little this and that. That was kind of what my whole thing was. Tom was really instrumental in my finding my own style—at least putting me on that path.

You developed a lovely midrange tone. It is something I enjoy from Robben Ford as well.

Thank you. It's the Dumble [amplifier] kind of thing. I like the high articulation, lots of headroom in that midrange, which is really important. The guitar is a midrange instrument. I look for a midrange tone that is warm and pleasing to the ear. You can keep the volume up and not hurt people. You don't want to hurt anyone.

"Faux Mantini" sounds like an homage to Al Di Meola.

That song is the most frustrating thing I have ever recorded. I actually threw the guitar across the room. I'm used to getting something in one or two takes. That thing just took hours. I would get through 99 percent of it and screw the last note. I'm a big fan of playing the whole take. It was very frustrating for me but it was enlightening, to say the least. The real spark in that song was my actually throwing the guitar and doing one more take and nailing it. I used a Martin D-28. It was an old one that I threw, so I felt bad. I play this song live every once in a while.

It's certainly a different style than the blues.

I listened to a lot of Al Di Meola, Paco De Lucia [*Friday Night in San Francisco*], and all those guys. I was listening to a lot of that. I said it would be cool to put a song on the record that kind of has that thing going. We did and it was one of the fan favorites. I just thought it was a track that would be there, the sorbet at the end of the record. But most of the fans really love it.

You have so many different visions of how to play the instrument. How is it that you seem to have such open ears for playing different styles?

I'm just a music fan. I think that's my biggest asset or my biggest curse. Guys who are just into one thing tend to have, in some respect, slightly more successful careers because it's just one thing over and over again. For me, I really enjoy all music. I get inspiration from everything. So I'm, like, it would be kind of cool to put this thing on there. Yesterday the band had a two-day bus ride from Aspen to Virginia Beach. I got this thought in my head: Wouldn't it be a cool thing to end our show if we worked out a version of "Los Endos" from Genesis? We did it at the show last night and people went nuts. My whole thing is the people who come to see me play are not just blues fans; they have seen Genesis, they've seen Peter Frampton, they've seen George Thorogood or the Eagles or Zeppelin. And they've seen Muddy Waters. They are people like my dad. My dad is a great litmus test because he's into not only blues but CSN&Y. It's soup to nuts. That was the cool thing about being a product of the '60s—the fact that there was so much great music out there and you couldn't not notice it all because one day you had Neil Young put out a classic record, the next day Zeppelin would release one. That's kind of the mentality that I subscribe to. That's why my records as a whole touch on so many different styles.

Are there musicians like that out now? Does that exist today?

I think guys like Derek Trucks are good like that. He touches on so many different styles from Delta blues to Indian scales. He has a very cool thing going. There's a bunch of cool guys. I think music on the radio today by and large sounds all the same to me. I could not tell you the difference between the bands Hinder, Nickelback, or whoever. I can't discern the audible difference. Zeppelin didn't sound like Free. The Faces sounded different than Chicago, but they were all accepted.

Today if you don't fit that very strict mold of what can be played on radio, you are kind of left in the dark. You have a bunch of guys chasing the same nickel and making records that sound exactly the same. The records are made by the same producers in the same studios, using the same equipment. When you introduce a new artist you say: What do they sound like? Who do they sound like? Nobody sounded like Hendrix when he came out. He was Jimi Hendrix. A lot of it was word of mouth. You have to see this left-handed guy who dresses so wild and plays this wild guitar. That's all they could say about him. They didn't say he sounded like Scotty Moore because he didn't. That's the problem with the music business today…music in general. The record companies are not signing many records. I think it's partly the artists' fault. How many records have I bought that I thought were going to be cool—that I bought for one song and the rest was just filler. There's too much filler and not enough interest in making a record deep. Now, on Jeff Beck's *Truth*, there ain't a bad song on there. I love "Let Me Love You," even down to his version of "Greensleeves." "Ol' Man River" killed me every time. Rod Stewart sang it so beautifully. There you go. Guys today don't sing like guys. I think they sing like girls. They are concentrating too much on being sensitive singer/songwriters and not concentrating enough on portraying real emotion when they sing. When Solomon Burke sang in the '60s, you knew he was there. When B.B. King sang, you knew he was there. Same with Rod Stewart and Paul Rodgers. You knew these guys meant it and you could feel it. With Elvis Presley, you could feel it. It's soul. It's blues based. There are some great singers out there; don't get me wrong. Kelly Carkson is really good. I think she sings blues based and is very soulful.

Did you like the Kelly Clarkson–Jeff Beck song from *American Idol*?

Yeah, I thought it was awesome.

For "Had to Cry Today," why did you change the last part of the lick that was originally a B-flat to a G?

I had to re-arrange it because when I do a cover song I don't like to do verbatim versions. The best version's already been done. You want to hear Steve Winwood sing that.

You changed the classic riff.

We changed it slightly. It actually grooved better with the band at the time. I think it was the bass player who did the variation and I actually kind of dug it. It was a song that we ended our live shows with for a long time. We played it so much we wanted to record it. Nobody else ever did.

I noticed a lot of key changes.

Yeah, there are. The solo modulates to G, which is basically the original key of the song.

The chorus is in F-sharp. What do keys mean to you as you're playing?

It's the old *Star Search* key change. It always works. Modulating the solo helps a lot.

Do specific keys mean different things to you as a guitar player?

Yeah, they do. When you go from E to G you don't have all those open strings to deal with. It sounds a little bit hot. As you go up, keys sound better or worse. To solo in D always has that really hot tone; so does G.

What guitar did you use for the recording

I used a '62 Gibson ES-335.

"If Heartaches Were Nickels" is the slow minor blues, the money shot.

That was a song Warren Haynes wrote for my album. It came out brilliantly. It is one of the biggest songs that I've ever done. We still play that live. The big thrill was when Gregg Allman sang on it. He sang great.

Did everybody fly in their parts, or were they there?

They came in at different times. Gregg came in and then Leslie [West] came in and we were there. Warren didn't play on it. He was overseas with Gov't Mule.

This song is your meat and potatoes.

Pretty much the make or break moment. I believe I used an old '63 Strat for this one. We do it acoustically live now.

The mark of a great song is that it doesn't have to be electric to be electrifying.

Exactly. The mark of a great song is it doesn't need a band. You can just play it and sing it or just sing a verse or a melody. That's the mark of the true classic stuff.

Can you be creative on demand?

Not really; I don't think so. I don't know if I can be creative in general. It's yet to be determined. Be creative

on demand, like schedule a writing session tomorrow at noon and walk in cold and be creative? Yeah, you can.

What about your solos?

That's improvising. I'm a good improviser. You can categorize that.

You talked about tone. Did you have to work on it a lot?

Oh, yeah. I work on tone every day, experimenting with different types of gear, different amps and speakers and cables, and working on my technique. You can create different tones just by having different technique. Lightening up on your picking creates a different tone. Working on your finger style when you're soloing creates a better tone. Another good example would be basically just sitting there with the guitar. One of the greatest tone devices is the volume and tone control on the guitar. It's a forgotten universe. People go, "I just need a pedal" and leave the guitar volume and tone controls wide open. The tone on the guitar can be varied.

Where is the spark in "Miss You, Hate You"?

In the writing of it. I think I used somebody's Martin acoustic guitar. I wrote it at somebody's house. It took me 45 minutes and to this day it's the closest thing I've ever had to a hit. I felt good about it. It was the record company who noticed it. The original version is seven minutes long. There's an 82-bar solo at the end. So I wasn't looking particularly for radio.

This has a great example of your beyond-the-blues soloing.

It's a pop song. But Clapton did pop songs and he played blues over them. Having different changes, the pentatonic thing takes on a different thing.

Billy Gibbons once told me that too often blues is treated like it's this museum. That's okay but you've got to open the windows and throw open the doors and let the fresh air run through, so you can keep it fresh and new.

Exactly. I'm a firm believer in that. To play blues like it was 1925, I don't believe there is a huge market for that. I think there is more of a market for blues with a different spin, a different take. It really is a combination of different styles and bringing it to the masses. We're talking about the people that Clapton and ZZ Top attract. B.B. King brings it to the masses.

When you were young and hanging with Danny Gatton, were you aware enough to listen to what he told you?

I was a shy kid. People have had to kind of say: Okay Joe, you can play. Over the years I've actually gotten somewhere out of the "I'm not worthy" complex. When I was a kid, Dan was a good friend and we used to hang out. He let me play his Telecaster and he would go back and say: Hey kid, you know nothing about Scotty Moore; you know nothing about Howard Reed; you know nothing about Duane Eddy, and Link Wray, Doc Watson, and Wes Montgomery. So all of sudden this whole world of different players was an explosion of influences that came in within a year. I was like wow and it set me on a path.

Did you know yours was a rare experience?

For me it was. Here is my really good guitar-playing friend Dan. I didn't realize he was going to go down as such a legend. I knew he was one of the best guitar players in the world. But you don't know how history is going to judge people. To me that time was very spe-

cial. Danny was just one of the nicest people in the world and one of the gems of the earth. A dream is to be a great musician, but to be a great person is really the way to go. The way I judge people, B.B. King is the ultimate example. There's not a mean bone in his body. He is the most kind, gentle soul that you're ever going to meet, and he is also one of the most talented people in the world and an icon of music.

Tell me a little about "My Mistake."

That was my kind of delving into more rock stuff. More like *Behind the Sun*–era Clapton. The spark was probably in the recording. I actually never have performed that song live.

I loved "A New Day Yesterday." Jethro Tull's *Stand Up* is a great album.

Stand Up is an awesome record. It was the first with Martin Barre [on guitar] as opposed to Mick Abrahams. I love that riff. It's all about that riff. When I first heard that song I could really hear it as a 12/8 blues. Playing it live, it's one of the most popular songs we have. People just love that riff. This was on my first album. I was a little tyke of 20 years old.

The recorded version is very good, but the version on the live DVD—in fact, that whole live DVD—is one of the best I've heard.

Thank you. We record once every 12 or 13 months, but we play almost 200 nights a year. We have more practice in the live thing than the other thing.

Did you do any overdubs on the DVD?

No, it was live. We did this for Rock Palace and they did a great job mixing it, too.

"Revenge of the 10 Gallon Hat" is your country chicken pickin' song.

This is my Danny Gatton tribute. I wrote that song as a challenge to my band at the time. They said, "Oh, we can play anything." "Okay, play this." It was actually a lot of fun. It was just the way I phrase country. If Brent Mason did an interpretation he would place his notes in a certain place. That kind of thing is up to the individual player. I played it a couple of times. I have my live rig set for everything except that really twangy compressed two Twins and an Echoplex thing. I don't carry the two Twins. If I had the Twins I could pull it off. The spark for this was really the writing. I wrote it on a '54 Esquire I still have.

"The River" brings out yet another style of playing.

I used an old '31 National. It was my take on "When the Levee Breaks." It's a cool song. I like the open F thing. We were talking about keys. Tuning your guitar from open E to open F creates a hotter tone. It's a little more vibrant, has a little more vitality to it. Plus it's easier for me to sing. So I'm making up this really intellectual reason why I did it that way only to boil it down to the fact that I couldn't sing it in E; I could sing it better in F. We moved "Burning Hell" up from E to F after that because it had more life to it. It had more fire. This was just a riff that I came up with. I like this. I wrote it very quickly. I wrote the lyric very quickly. The inspiration came from an old Mississippi Fred McDowell song that I saw on a DVD of *Live at Newport 1964*. What I wanted to do was a song like "When the Levee Breaks," but I didn't want to get sued. We do this song every three nights. It's in our rotation.

"So, It's Like That" is a classic shuffle.

It's a great song that my friend Mike Himelstein and I wrote. He has written a lot of my best songs. I needed a shuffle for the album. It ended up becoming the title track. I used a Clapton Strat. I love the midrange boost on that guitar. The spark was in the recording. We had had a bunch of wine at dinner—too much wine. We came back and we were like, "Hey, let's record it." We ended up doing one or two takes, but it had that drunken swagger that you only get when you are actually drunk and swaggering. That was the story. To me it sounds like the Faces because it was a drunken swagger tune. It could have easily been too white- or Wonder Bread shuffly.

What are some of the characteristics of British blues that you found so attractive?

Just the sophistication of it, and the fact that it didn't sound all the same. If you listened to a Ten Years After record, not one song sounded identical to the others. If you listened to Jethro Tull or Free, there was melody where, I thought, the American blues lacked a melody. The blues purists are going to string me up for that one, but it's true.

Often the best playing is when you're relaxed rather then fully prepared and trained and waiting for the red light to go on. When you are laid back, it flows out of you rather than springs out of you. That's why very often people play well as a guest on a record. There is no pressure.

Yeah, that's the whole thing. You are more comfortable in the studio.

When are you at your best?

When I'm tired and relaxed and devoid of any personal problems with the girlfriend or any business thing. When I'm only thinking about playing and I'm tired and relaxed. The tired part is important. I'm tired the right amount pretty often, but being devoid of any personal problems or anything business related is rare. It's all normal stuff. But I think I am able to shut it off more, before my mind starts wandering. I am probably diagnosed ADD.

Do you try to cut yourself off a couple of days before recording?

Nah. You have to live life and it is what it is. I know when a good take is a good take. So if I can get a good take in two takes, then we're done. If it takes me five takes, then so be it. I'll get there; it may take me longer. Kevin Shirley is brilliant about that, by the way. He really can get you something. He is awesome. He has produced my last two records.

"Woke Up Dreaming" I thought of as an acoustic Michael Hedges–like blues.

My friend Will Jennings and I wrote that song. Will and I love Jimmie Rodgers, the yodeling cowboy. He is a white guy from Texas, who is kind of like Robert Johnson playing blues country stuff. Very haunting. We are both fans of his lyrics and that kind of double entendre stuff. We said: Let's make a traditional blues but speed it up to hyper speed and see what happens when you add that kind of old-timey lyrics. That's what happens. It's one of my favorite tunes and everybody loved it. The biggest spark is probably the riff. Once you get grooving on that riff, you can see, even without any drums, people's heads start boppin'.

Did you spend time working on slide?

I spent a lot of time working on slide about five or six years ago when I realized I sucked at it. I had to re-evaluate the whole thing.

Do you re-evaluate your style playing on an acoustic guitar?

I think I'm a more original acoustic guitar player than I am an electric player. I don't have as many influences on the acoustic as I do on the electric. On the acoustic I just kind of pick it up and go. I'm not thinking of anybody when I'm playing. On electric I have been so influenced by other players that I think I actually sound more original when I play the acoustic. That's my theory.

BLUES DELUXE

Words and Music by
Jeffrey Rod

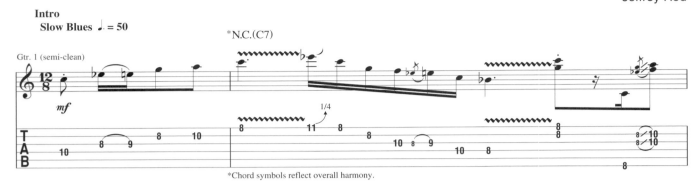

*Chord symbols reflect overall harmony.

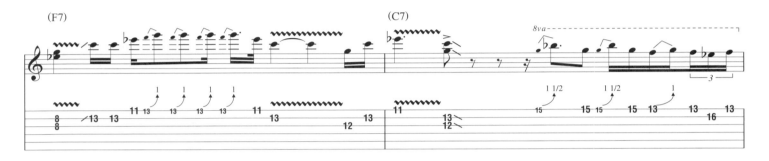

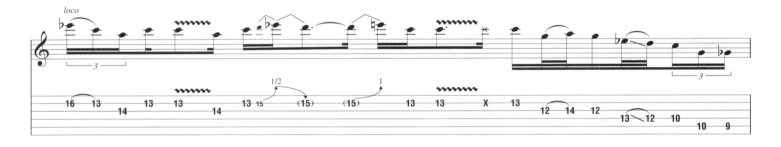

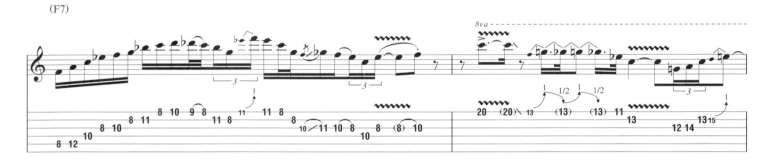

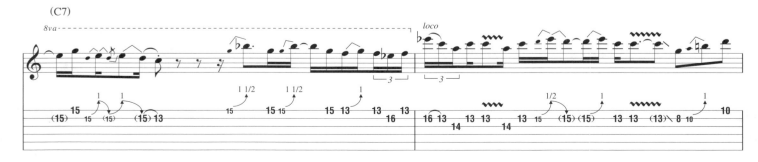

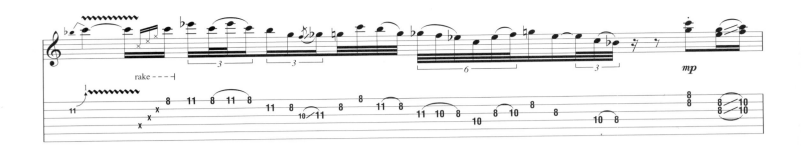

I don't know __ too __ much a - bout __ love, __ ba - by _____ now, __   but I sure __

N.C.(C7)

think I've got _____ it bad. ____ yeah. _____

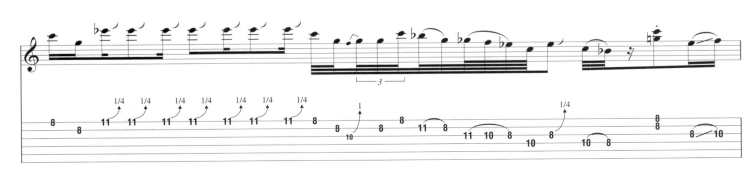

Some peo - ple say __ love is just a gam - ble.

Oo, what-ev - er it is, a - bout to drive _____ me

mad, __ yeah.

Hey, look out.

Verse

2. I sit here in my lone - ly room, __ now, __

tears _____ go - in'

N.C.(C7)

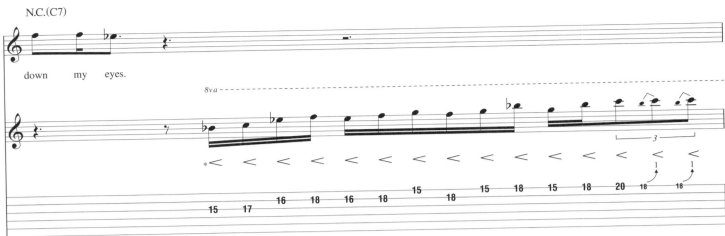

down   my   eyes.

*Vol. swells (next 2 meas.).

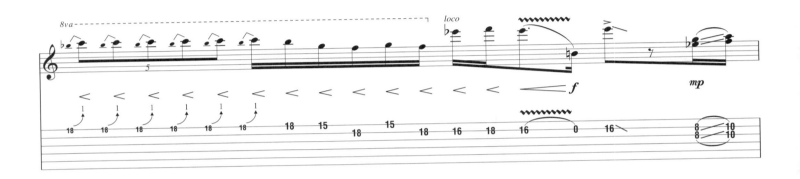

F9

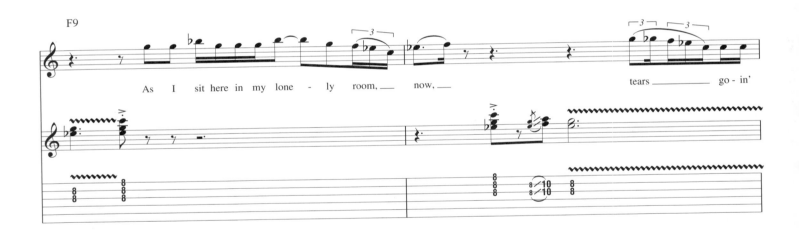

As   I   sit here in my lone - ly   room, ___   now, ___   tears _____ go - in'

N.C.(C7)

down   my   eyes.

*Vol. swells.

I won - der how you could treat me so low down and dirt - y.

You know what? Your heart must be made

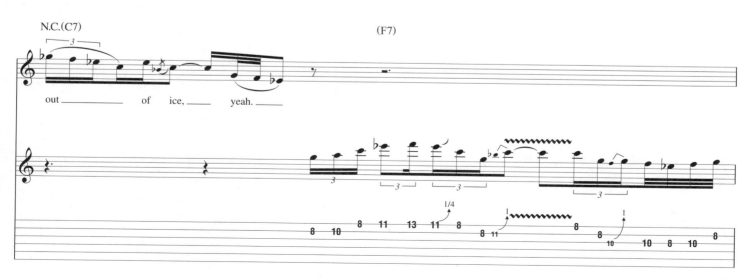

out of ice, yeah.

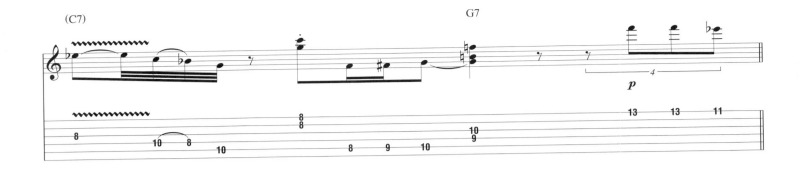

Guitar Solo

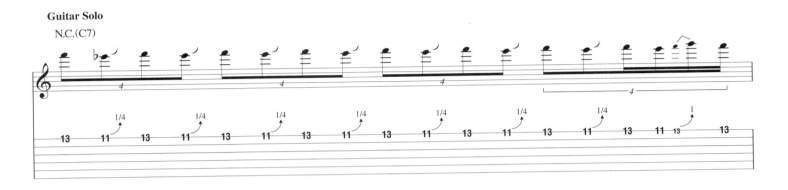

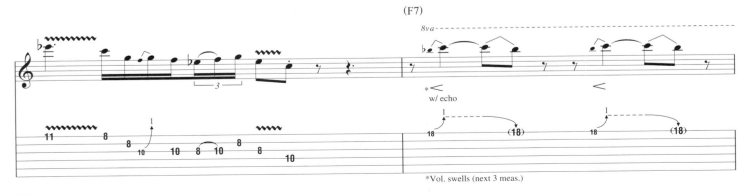

*Vol. swells (next 3 meas.)

16

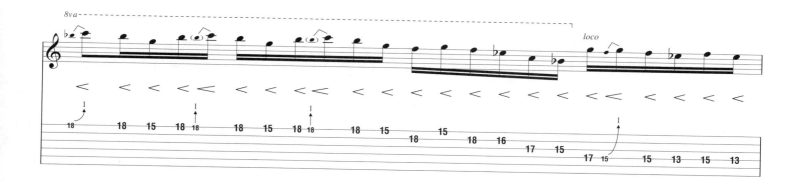

(C7)

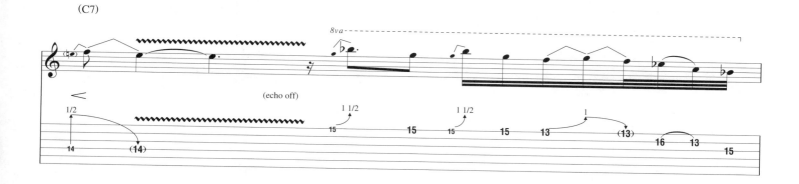

(G7)

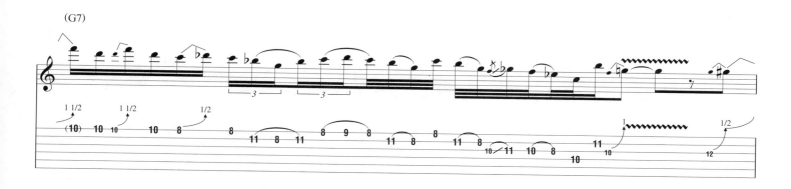

(F7)

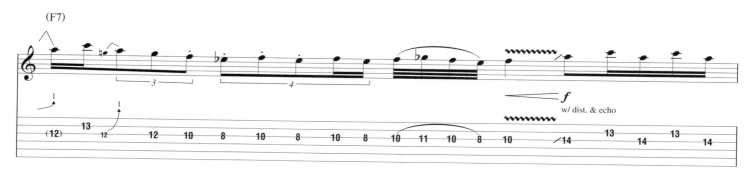

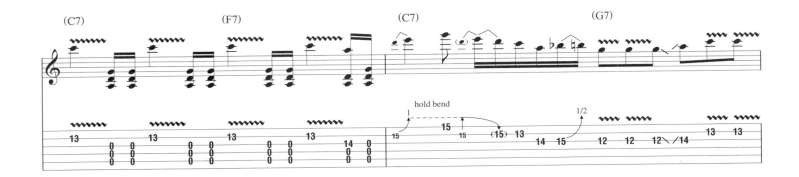

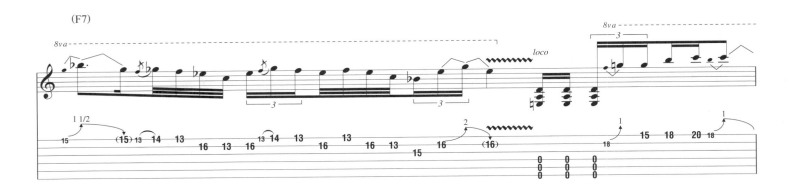

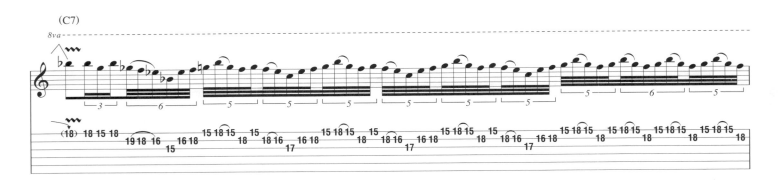

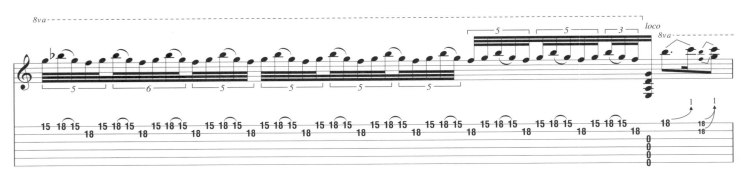

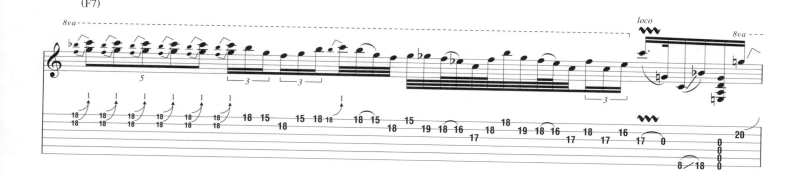

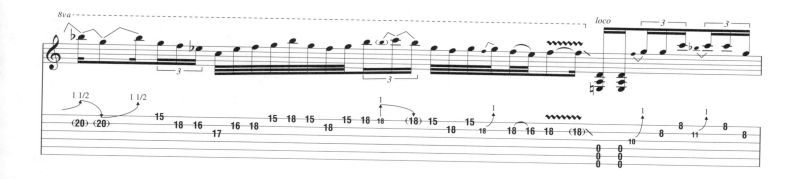

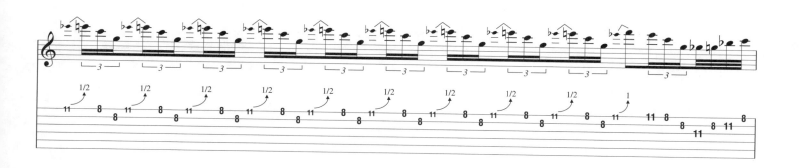

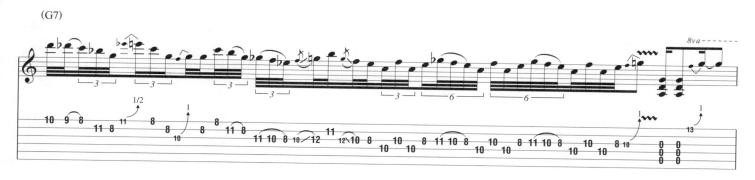

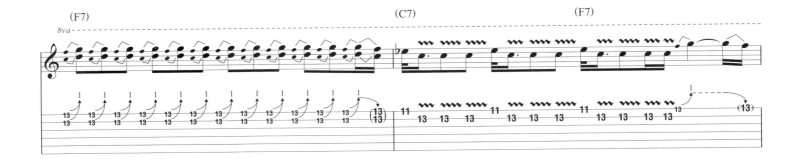

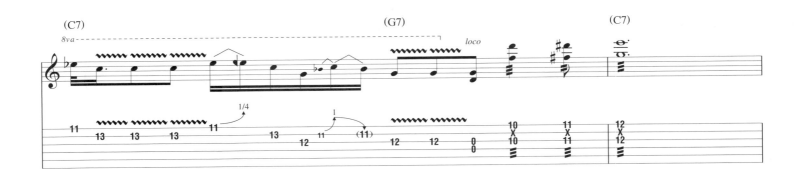

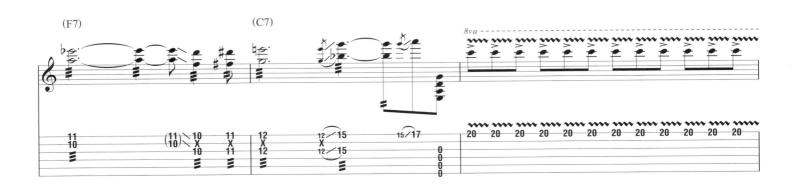

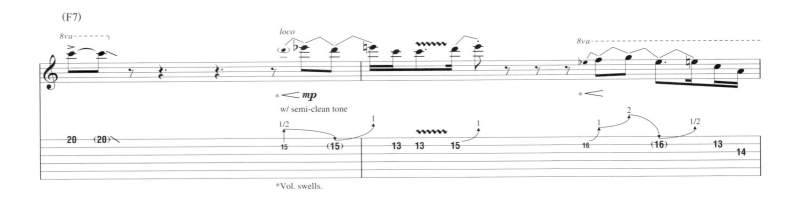

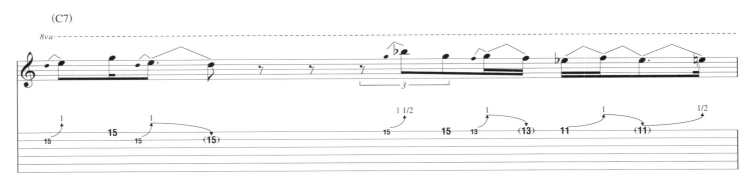

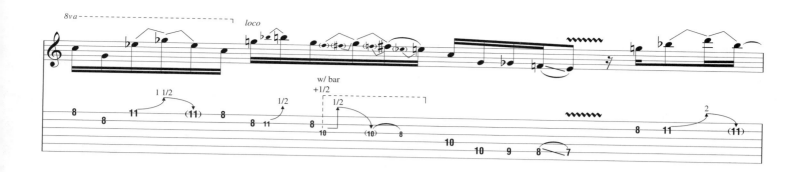

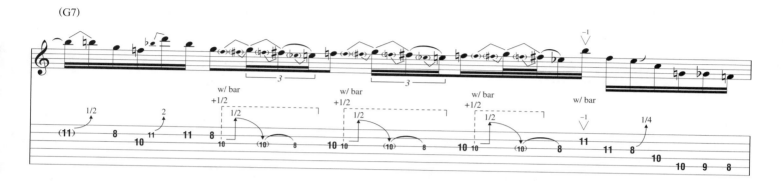

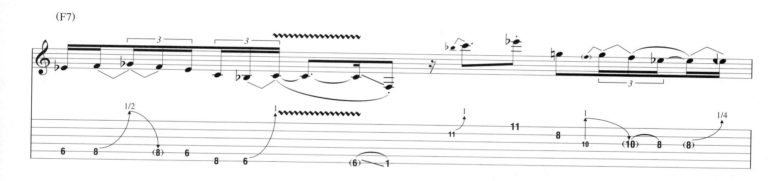

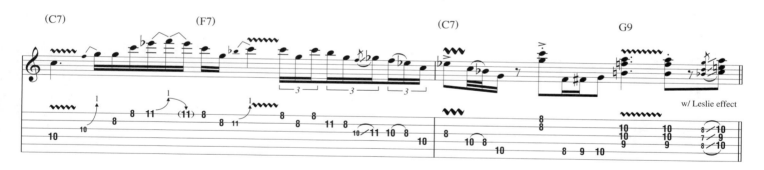

Verse

3. Some - times I ____ get so ____ wor - ried, ba - by ____ now, ____ you know, I wan - na

N.C.(C7)

sit down and cry _____ my - self to sleep. _____

*Vol. swells (next 2 meas.).

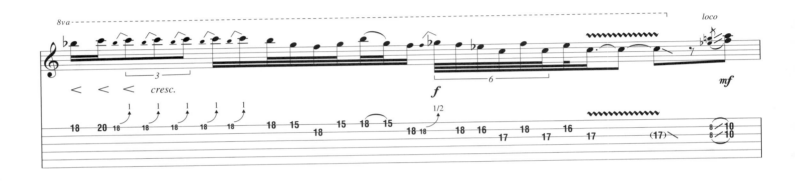

F9

Some - times I _____ get so _____ wor - ried, ba - by _____ now, _____ you know, I wan - na

N.C.(C7)

sit down and cry _____ my - self to sleep. _____

'Cause I don't know too much a-bout love, _____ babe, but I sure _____ think I, _____

sure _____ think I got _____ it bad, _____ yeah. _____

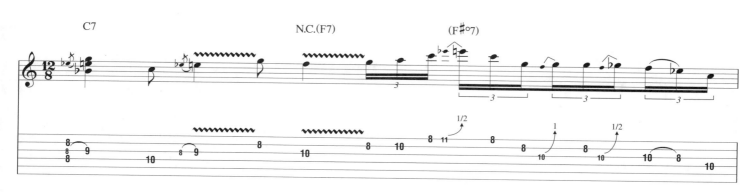

Free time

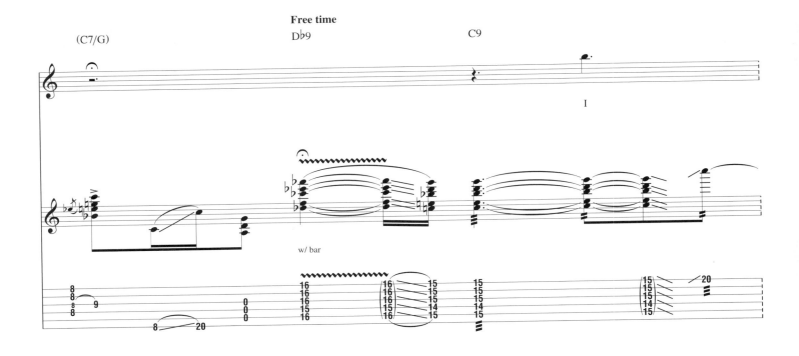

sure think I've got it bad, _____ yeah. _____

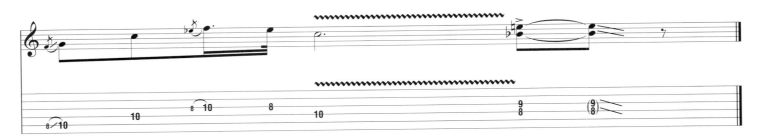

FAUX MANTINI

Words and Music by
Joe Bonamassa

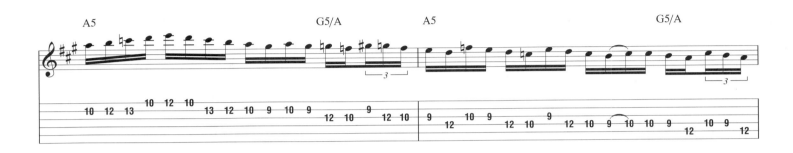

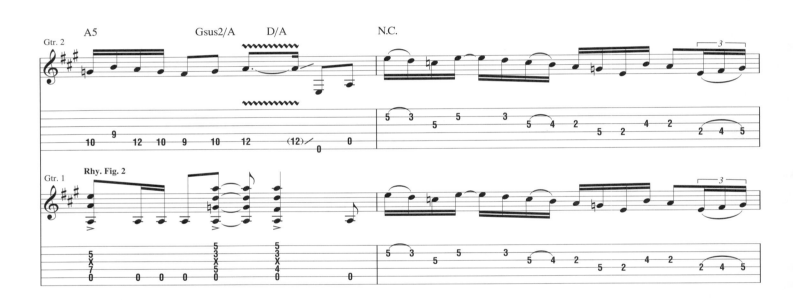

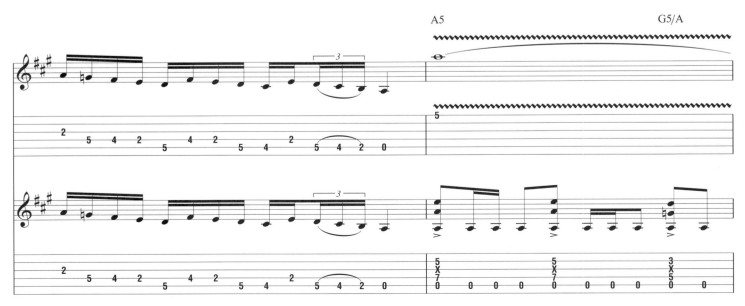

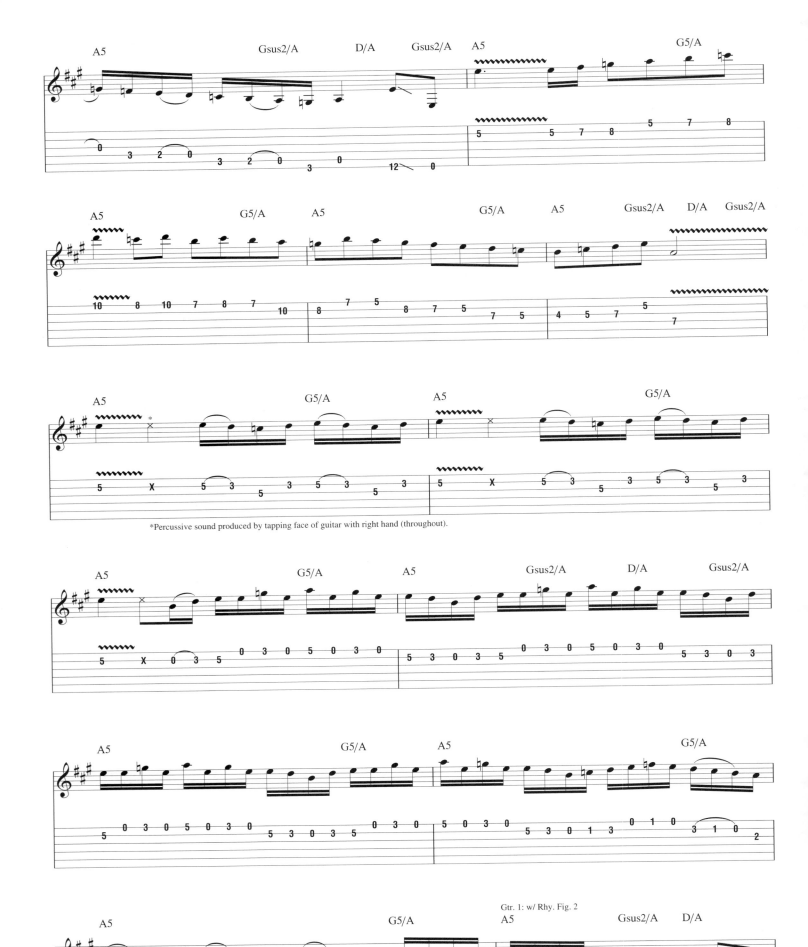

*Percussive sound produced by tapping face of guitar with right hand (throughout).

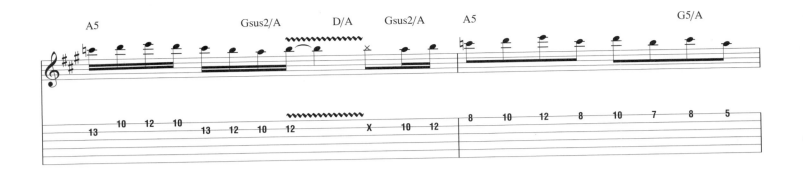

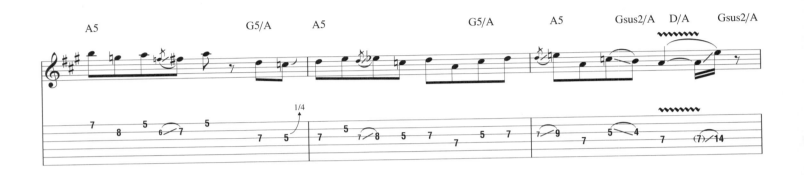

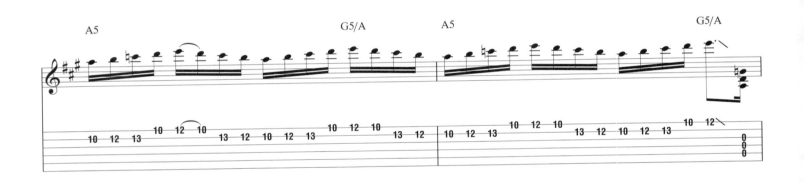

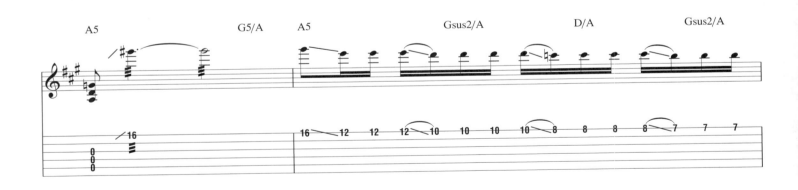

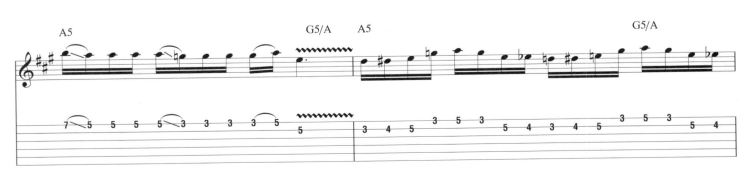

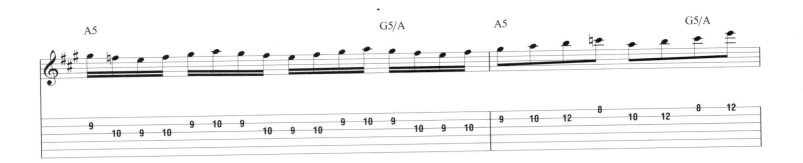

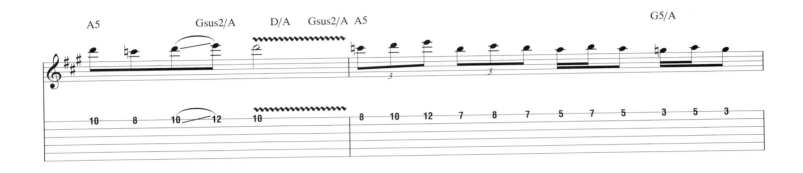

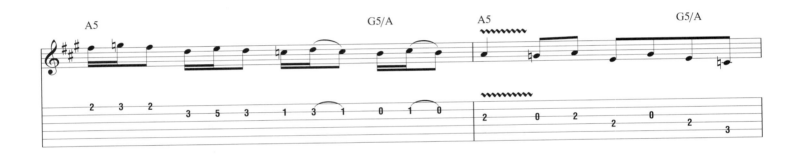

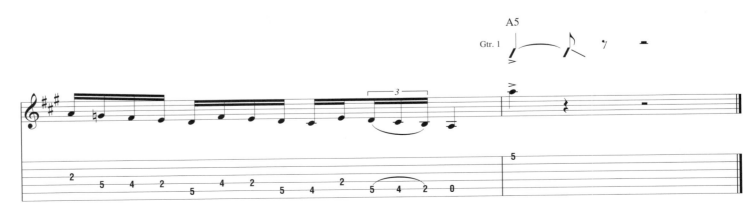

HAD TO CRY TODAY

Words and Music by
Steve Winwood

Intro
Moderate Rock ♩ = 92

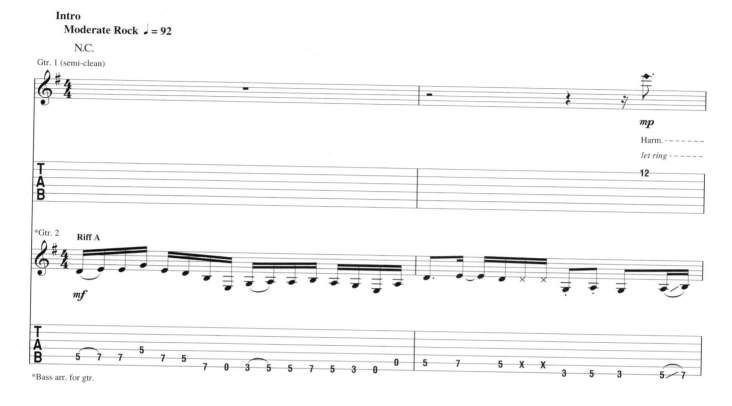

*Bass arr. for gtr.

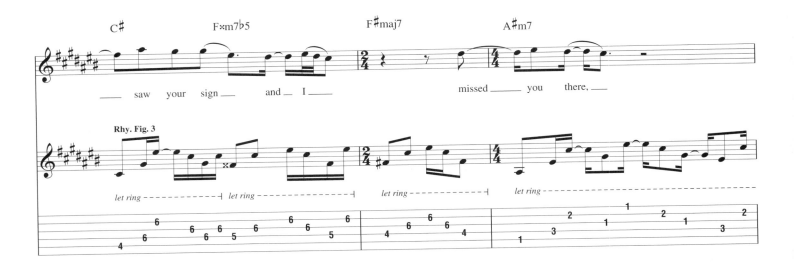

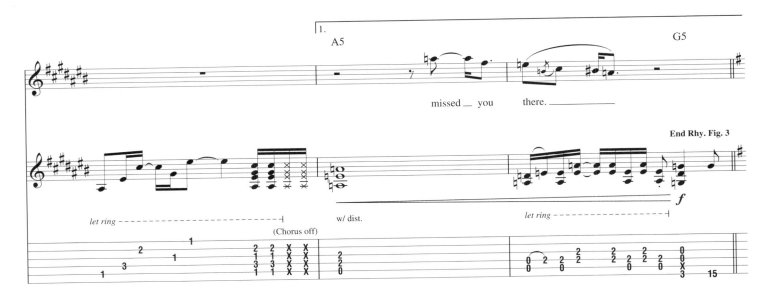

Interlude

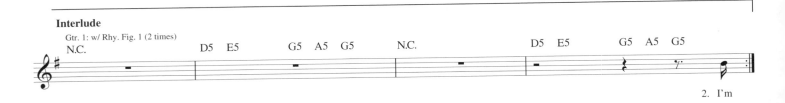

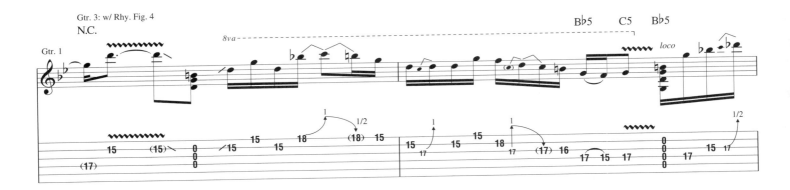

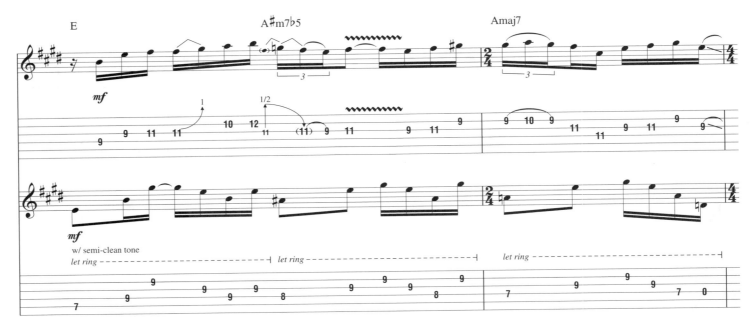

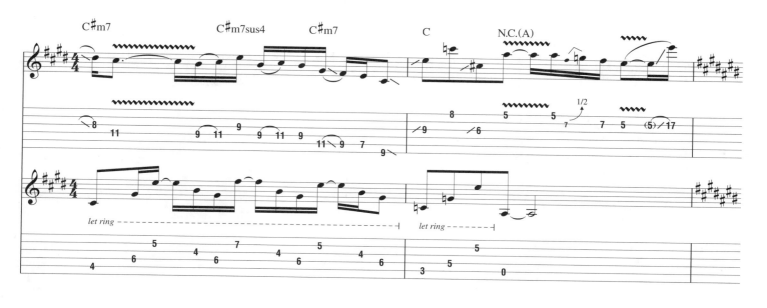

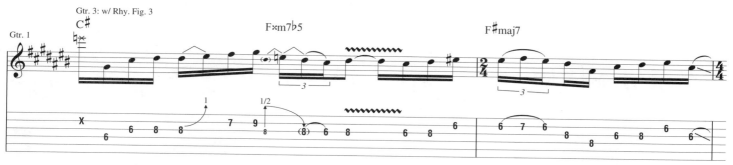

D.S. al Coda

Gtr. 1: w/ Rhy. Fig. 1 (2 times)

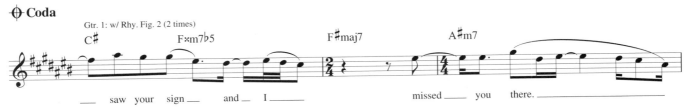

3. I'm

Coda

Gtr. 1: w/ Rhy. Fig. 2 (2 times)

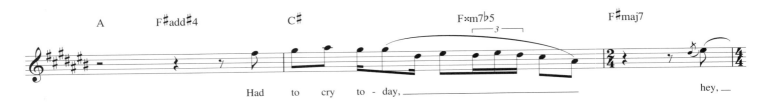

___ saw your sign ___ and ___ I ___ missed ___ you there. ___

Had to cry to-day, ___ hey, ___

yeah, ___ yeah. ___ Well, I ___

Gtr. 1: w/ Rhy. Fig. 3

___ saw your sign ___ and ___ I ___ missed ___ you there, ___

missed ___ you there. ___

Interlude

Gtr. 1: w/ Rhy. Fig. 1 (2 times)

Outro-Guitar Solo

Gtr. 1: w/ Rhy. Fig. 1 (16 1/2 times)

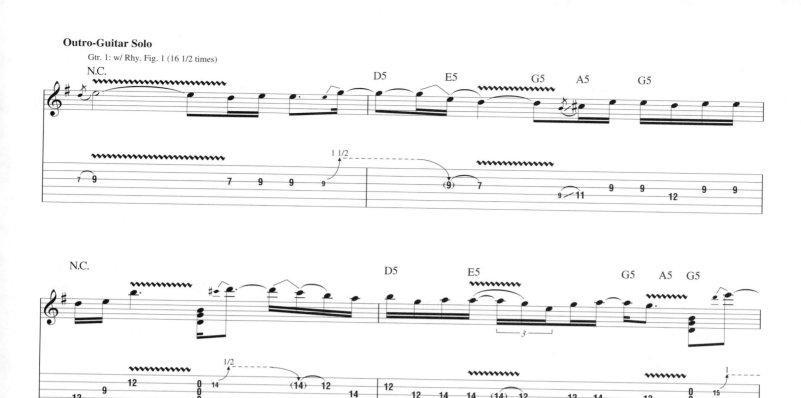

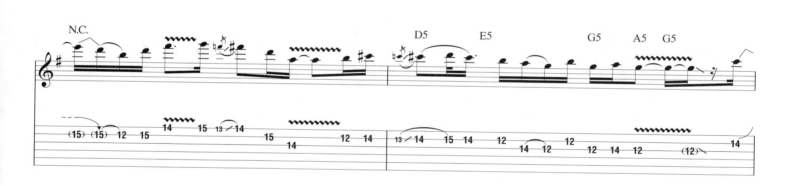

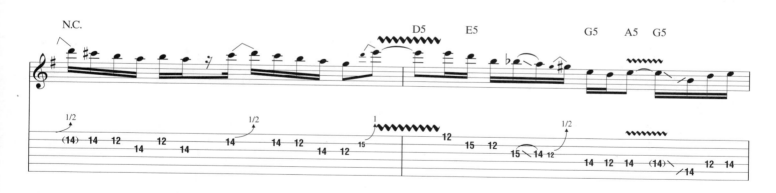

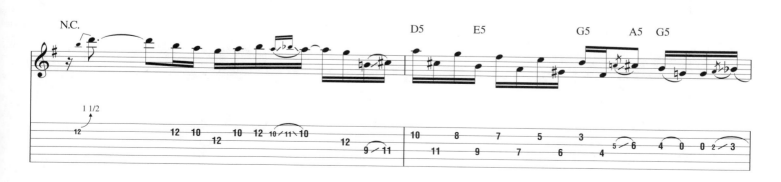

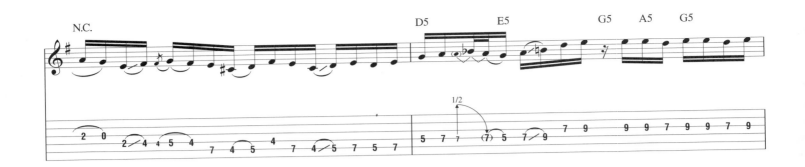

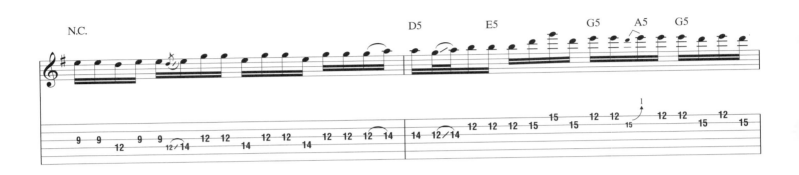

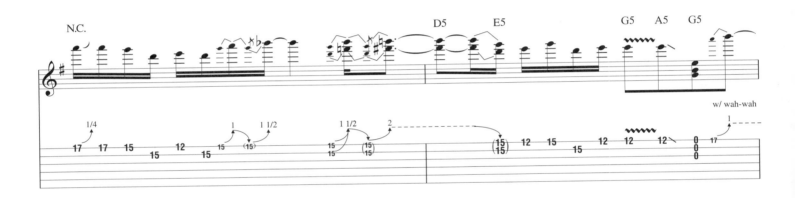

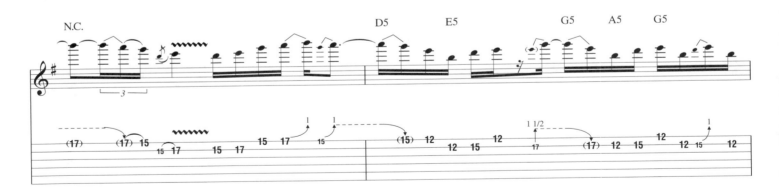

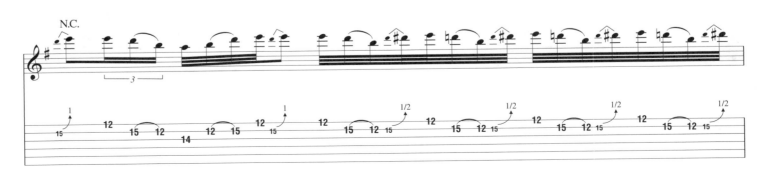

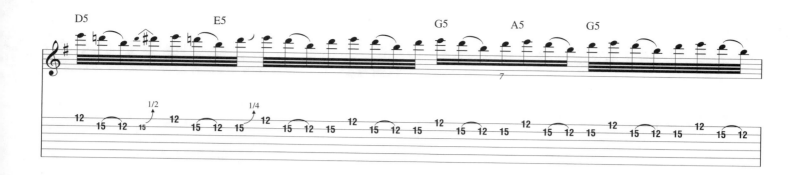

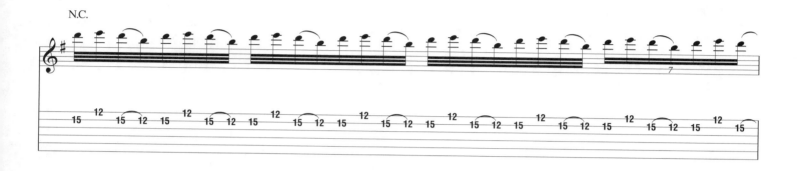

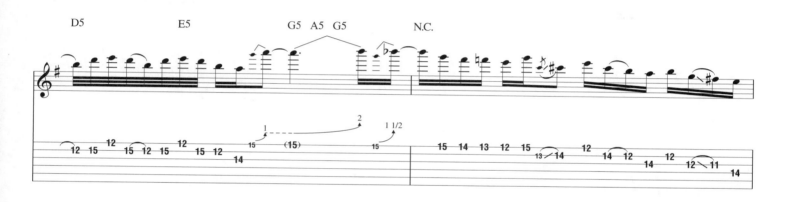

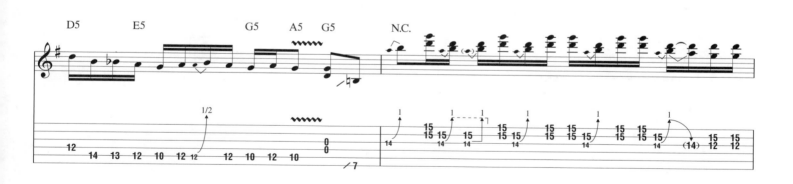

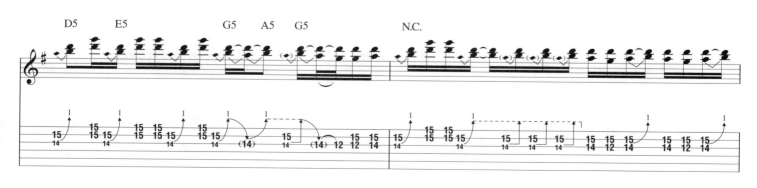

IF HEARTACHES WERE NICKELS

Words and Music by
Warren Haynes

dark. _____

Yes, if

℅ Bridge

2nd time, Gtrs. 1 & 2: w/ Rhy. Fill 2

wine _____ and pills were hun - dred dol - lar bills, I might keep you _ sat - is - fied. _____ And if

bro - ken dreams were lim - ou - sines, I might take you for a ride. _____ And all I can

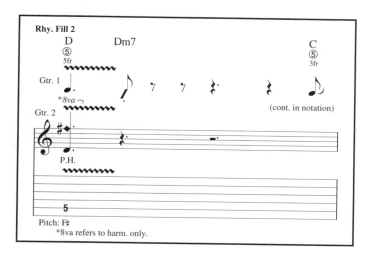

do _____ is think of you, _____ and wish you were here by my side. Yes, if

heart-aches were nick-els, _____ I'd be the rich-est _____ fool _____ a - live. Mm, _____

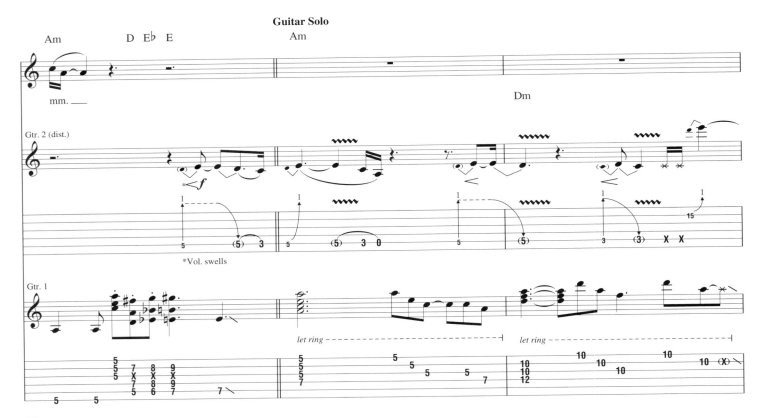

mm. _____

Gtr. 1: w/ Rhy. Fig. 3

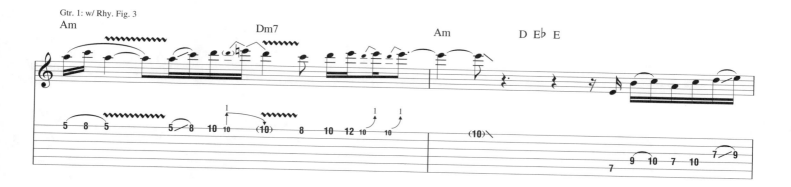

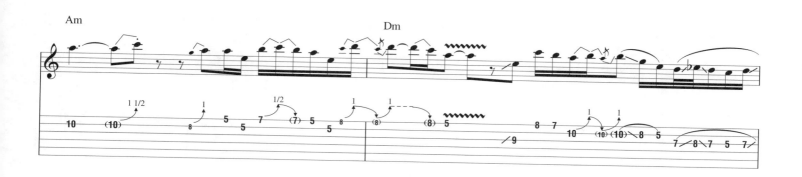

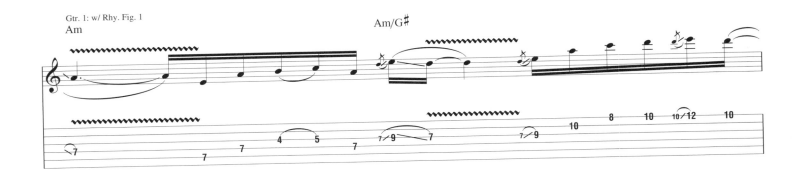

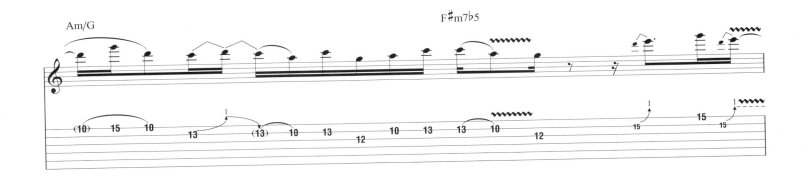

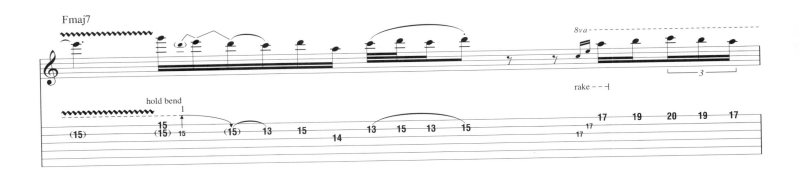

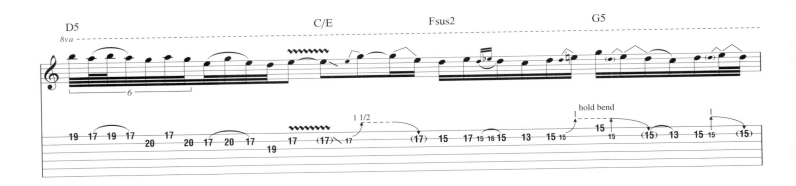

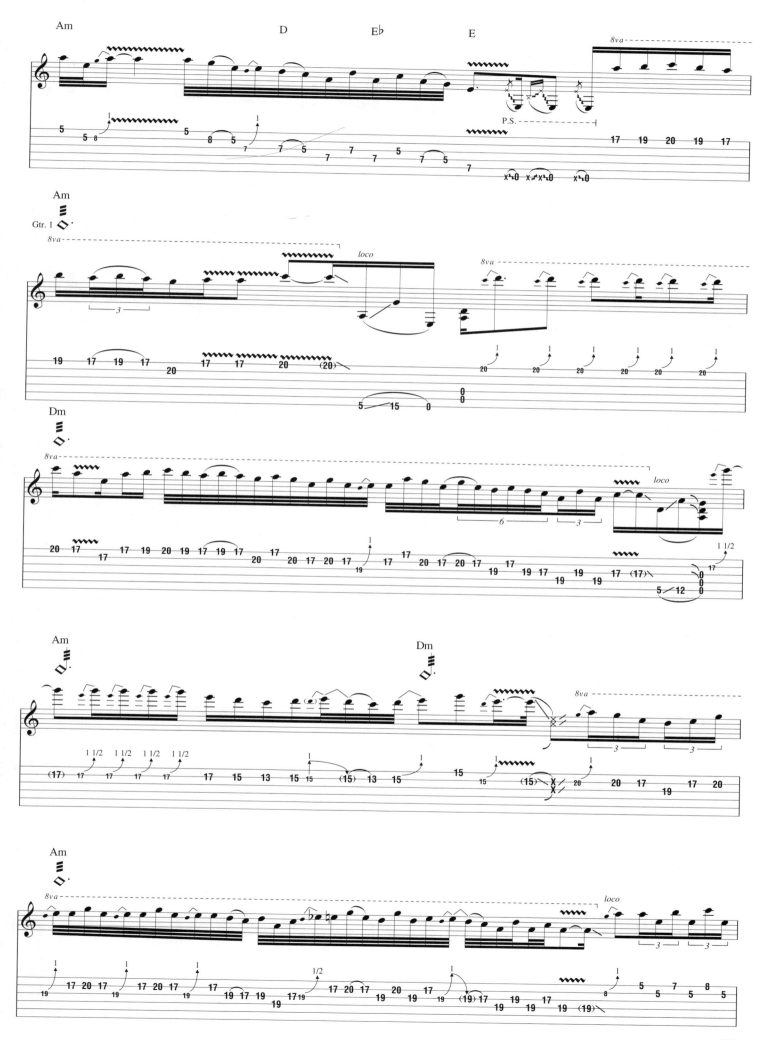

*Bass plays E.

**Bass plays E.

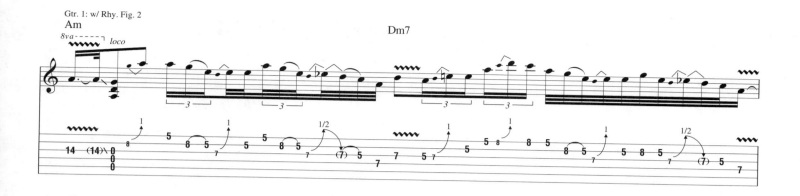

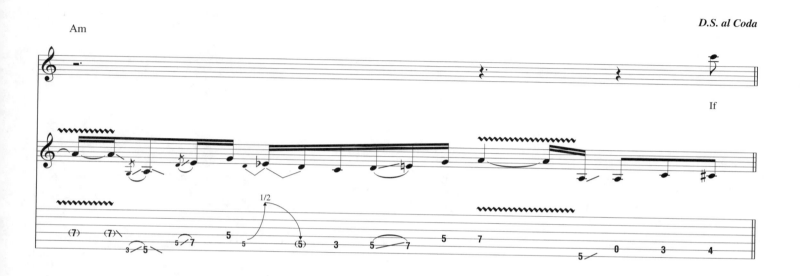

⊕ Coda

live, I'd __ be the rich-est fool a - live. _____

Freely

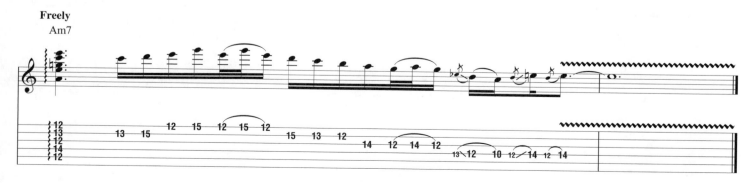

MISS YOU, HATE YOU

Words and Music by
Joe Bonamassa and Richard Feldman

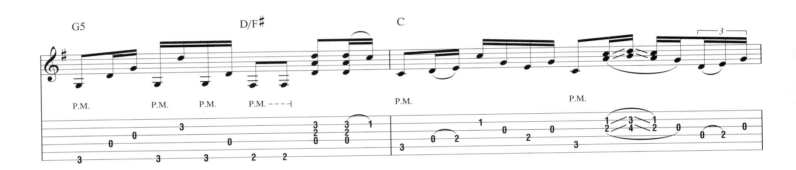

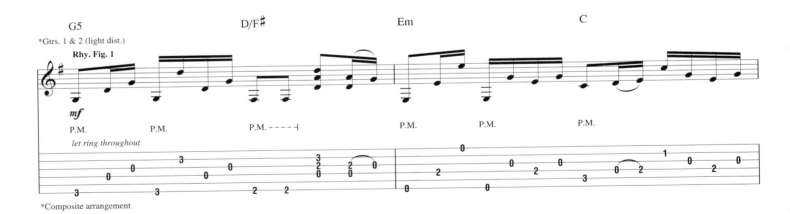

*Composite arrangement

Verse

1. I got a prob-lem burn-in' through ___ my veins.

I got a tat-too on ___ my arm ___ with your ___ name, _____

a rag-ing vi - rus burn-in' through ___ my skin.

Can you tell me — why — this has to end?

Interlude

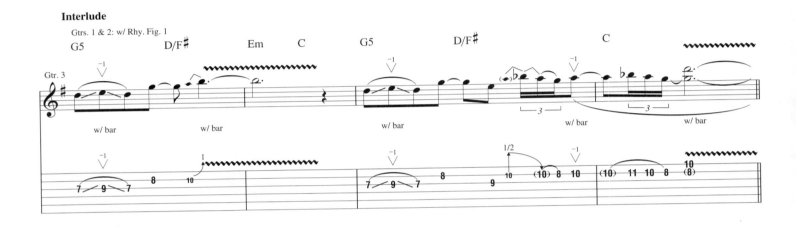

Verse

2. I did-n't mean — to hurt an-y-one.

Verse

3. I've been see-ing de-mons, __ and I've been see-ing saints. __

I've tried pre-tend-ing that I'm some-bod-y that I ain't. __

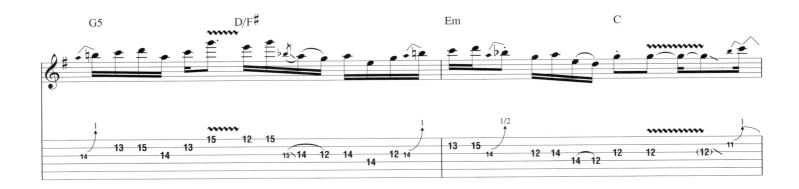

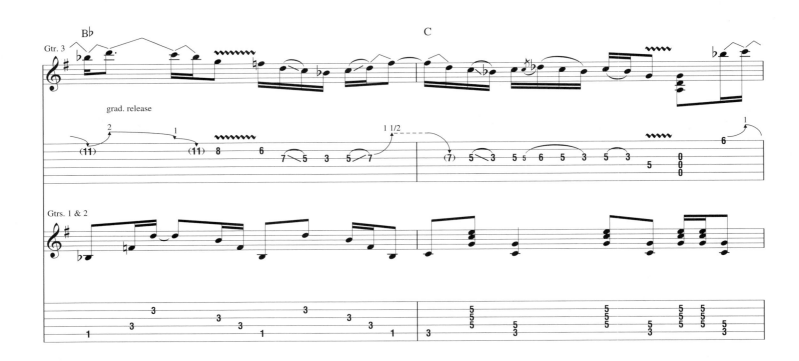

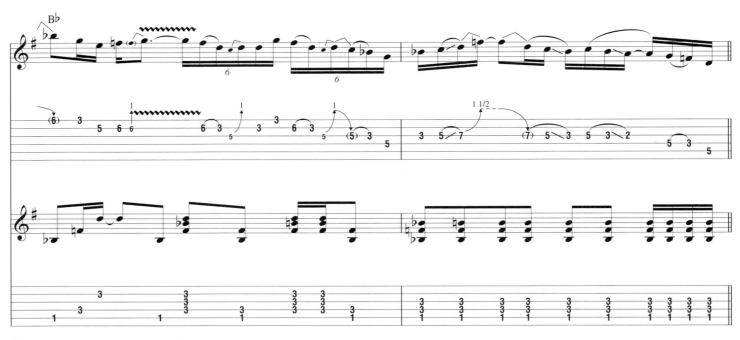

Outro-Guitar Solo

N.C.(Em)

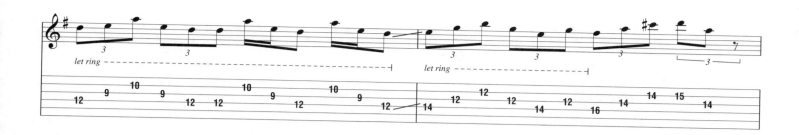
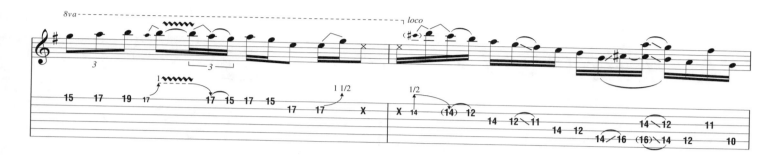

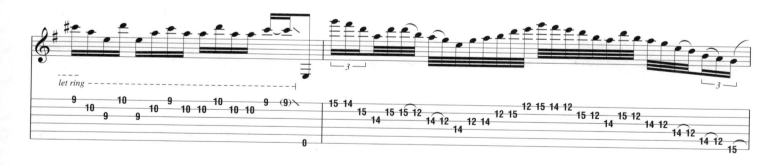

MY MISTAKE

Words and Music by
Joe Bonamassa and Mark Lizotte

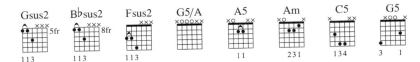

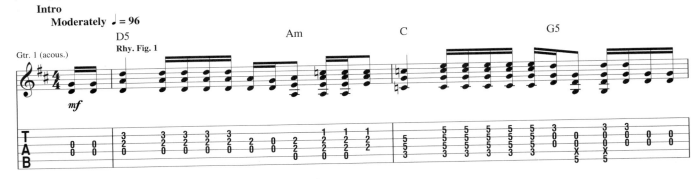

Gtrs. 1, 2 & 3: Drop D tuning, down 1/2 step:
(low to high) D♭-A♭-D♭-G♭-B♭-E♭
Gtr. 4: Tune down 1/2 step:
(low to high) E♭-A♭-D♭-G♭-B♭-E♭

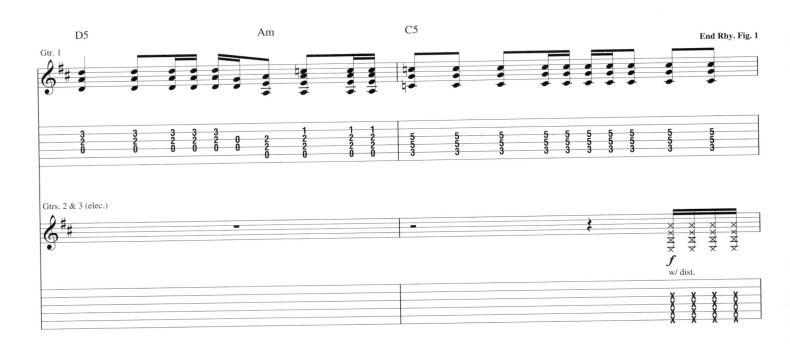

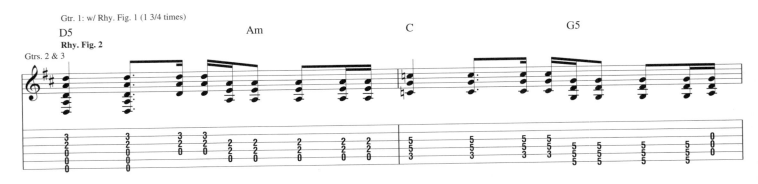

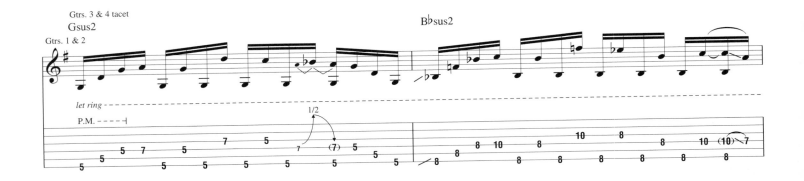

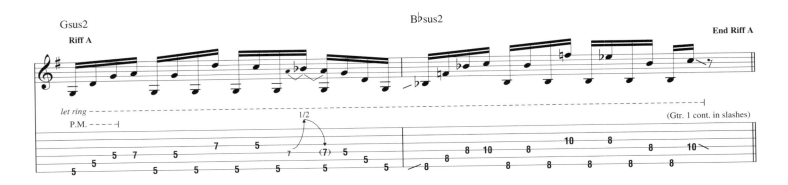

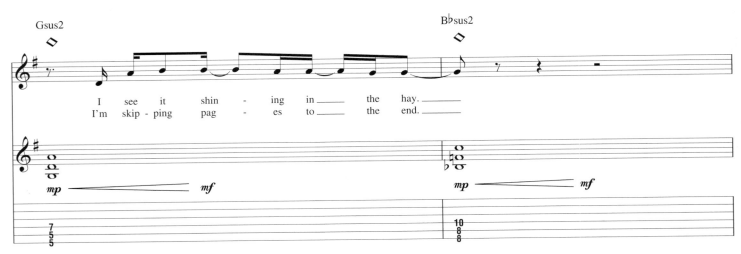

There's some - thing gold - en _____ in my _____ hands, _____ and
There's a sto - ry that ___ I'll nev - er ___ know: ___ and the

then I go ___ and let ___ it slip a - way. _____
one a - bout ___ the man ___ who makes _ a - mends. _____ With

Chorus
Gtr. 1: w/ Rhy. Fig. 1
Gtrs. 2 & 3: w/ Rhy. Fig. 2
3rd time, Gtr. 4 tacet

eyes that are bro - ken, my feel - ings are spo - ken. ___ It's time for the wa - ters to break. ___

1st time, Gtr. 1: w/ Rhy. Fig. 1 (1st 3 meas.)
1st time, Gtrs. 2 & 3: w/ Rhy. Fig. 3
2nd & 3rd times, Gtr. 1: w/ Rhy. Fig. 1
2nd & 3rd times, Gtrs. 2 & 3: w/ Rhy. Fig. 2

I know where I should ___ be, and I'm gon - na make ___ it there. ___ I

To Coda ⊕ |1.
Gtr. 1: w/ Rhy. Fill 1   Gtrs. 1 & 2: w/ Riff A   Gtr. 4: w/ Fill 1

won't let you be ___ my mis - take. _____

Fill 1
Gtr. 4

73

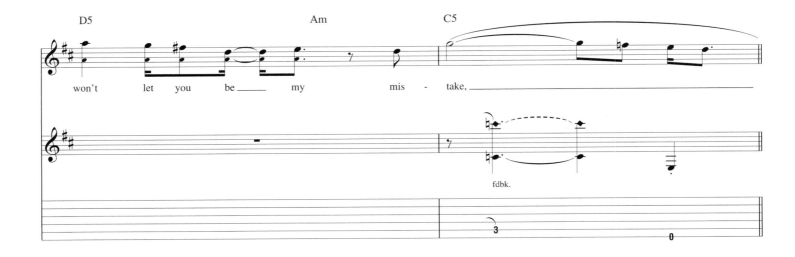

won't   let   you   be ____ my   mis - take, _____

Guitar Solo
Gtr. 1: w/ Rhy. Fig. 1 (7 3/4 times)
Gtrs. 2 & 3: w/ Rhy. Fig. 2 (6 times)

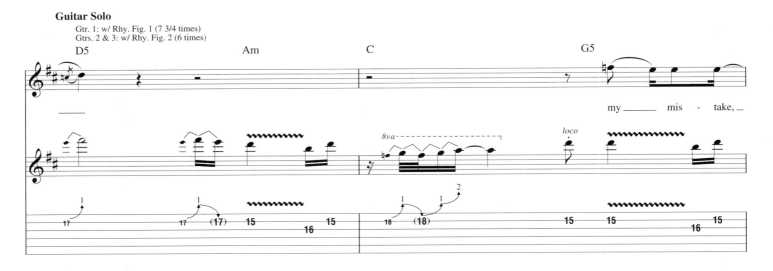

_____ my ____ mis - take, __

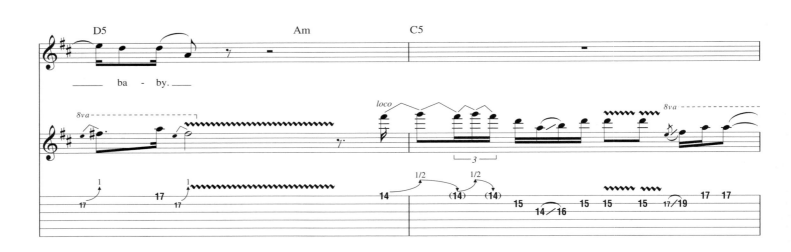

_____ ba - by. ____

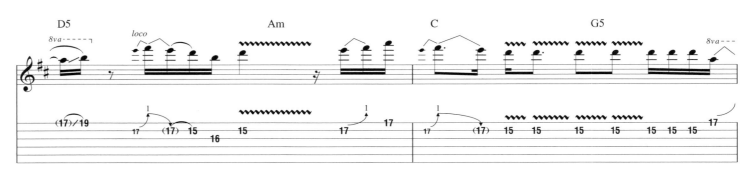

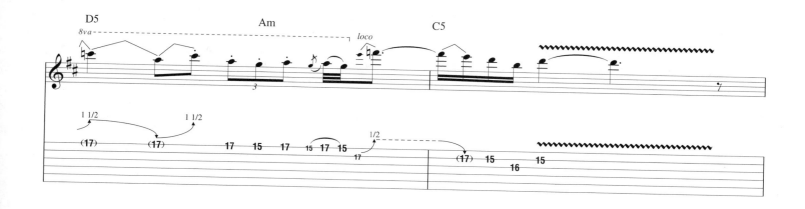

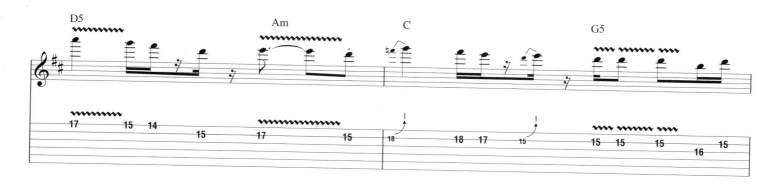

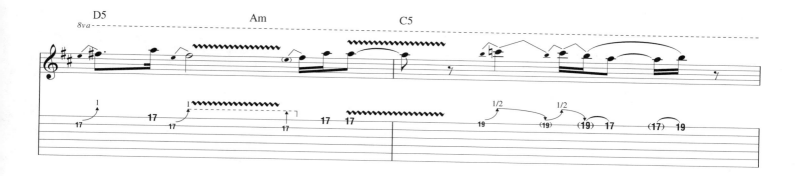

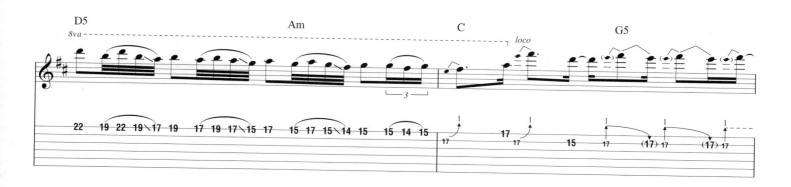

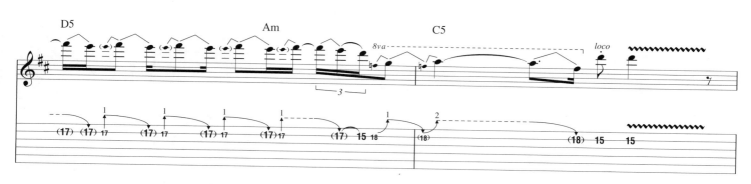

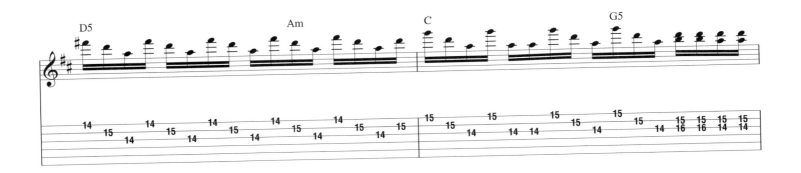

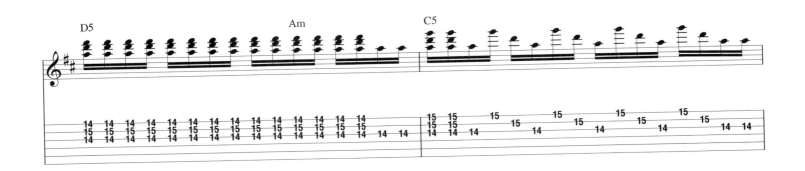

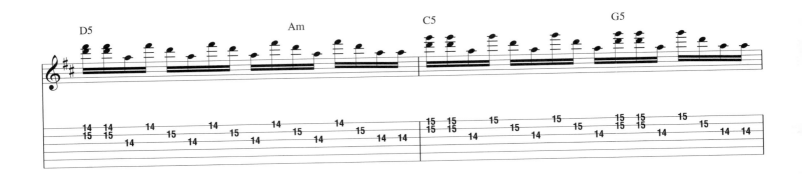

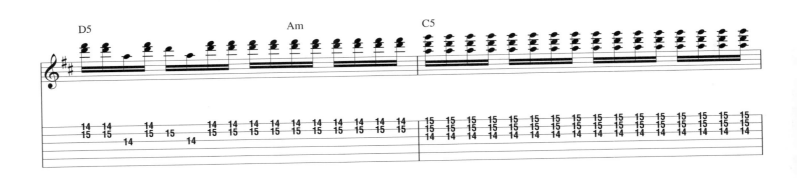

NEW DAY YESTERDAY

Words and Music by
Ian Anderson

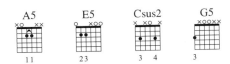

*Composite arrangement; Gtr. 2 (dist.)

Free time

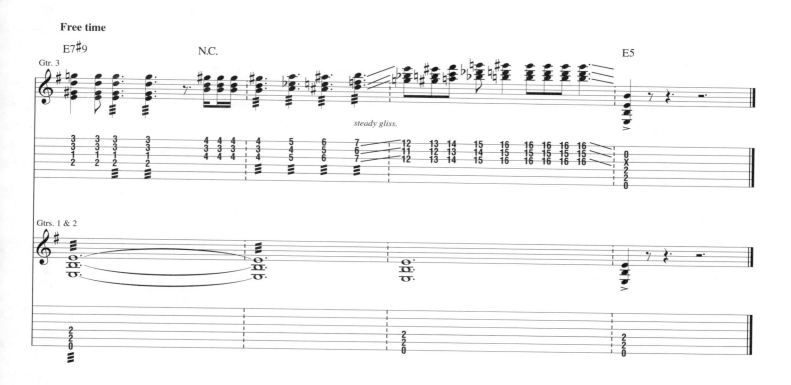

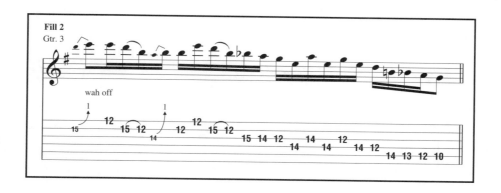

REVENGE OF THE 10 GALLON HAT

Words and Music by
Joe Bonamassa

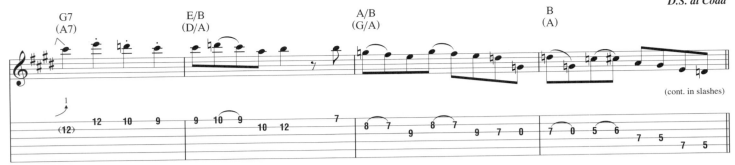

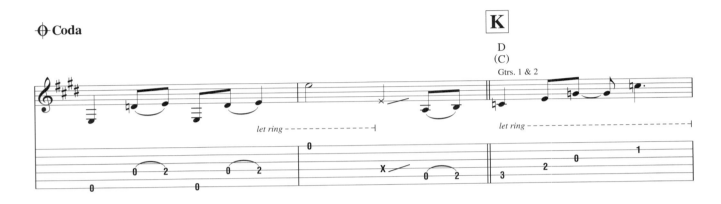

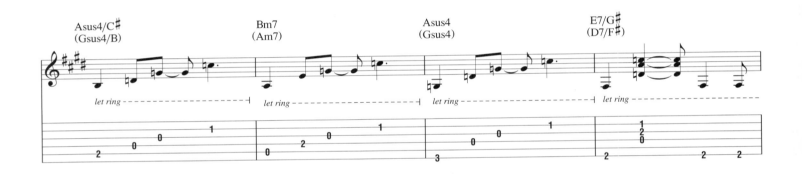

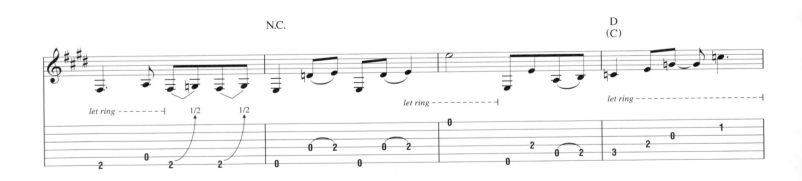

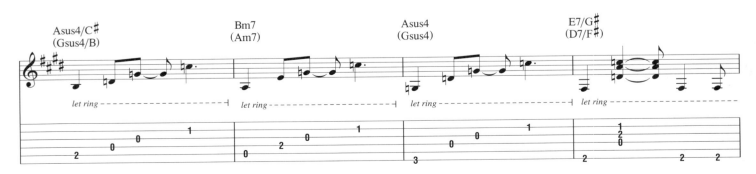

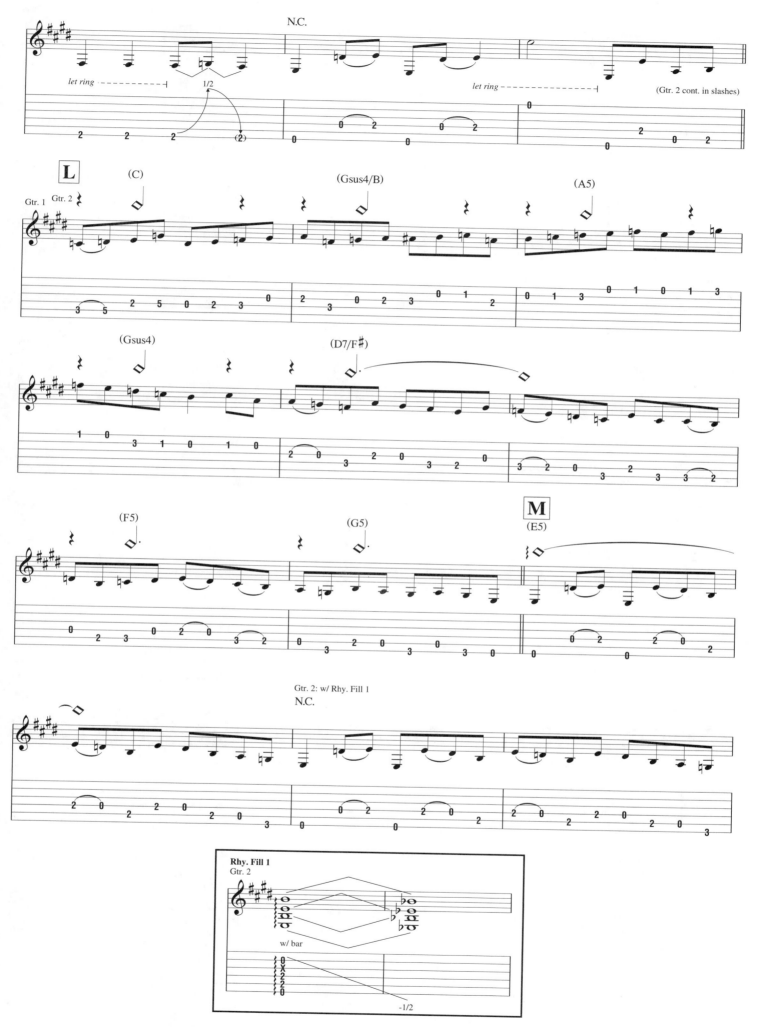

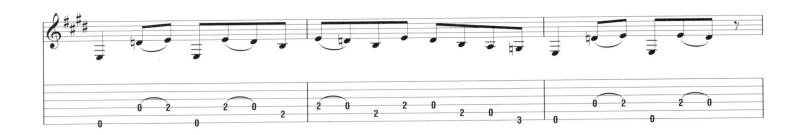

Gtr. 2: w/ Rhy. Fill 1

THE RIVER

Words and Music by
Joe Bonamassa and Robert Held

Open E tuning, up 1/2 step:
(low to high) F-C-F-A-C-F

Intro
Free time

N.C.

Gtr. 1
(National steel)

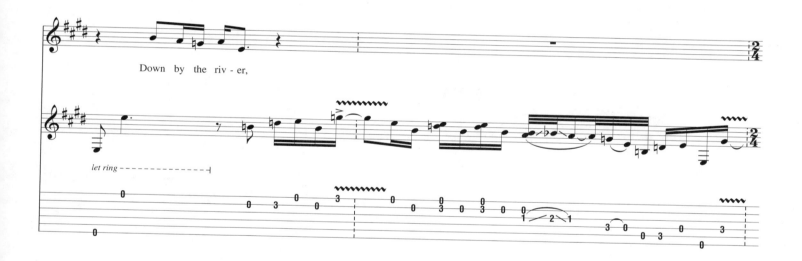

Down by the riv-er,

let ring -------------

that's where I broke down and cried. _____

let ring -------------

Down by the riv - er,

where I could just lay down and die. _____

E5/D

I'm go - in' down _____ to _____ the riv - er _____ for

long as I ___ can ___ stand. ___ Ma - ma told ___ me, "Son," ___ as she

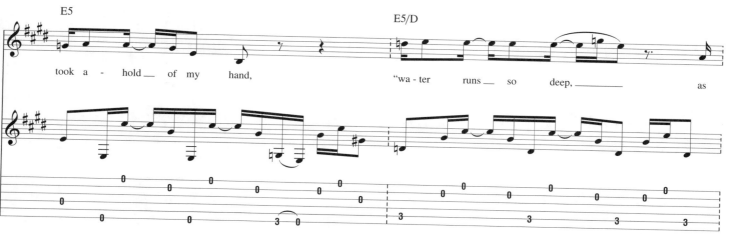

took a - hold ___ of my hand, "wa - ter runs ___ so deep, ___ as

deep as all ___ my pain." ___ Down ___ by ___ the riv - er, ___ hon - ey.

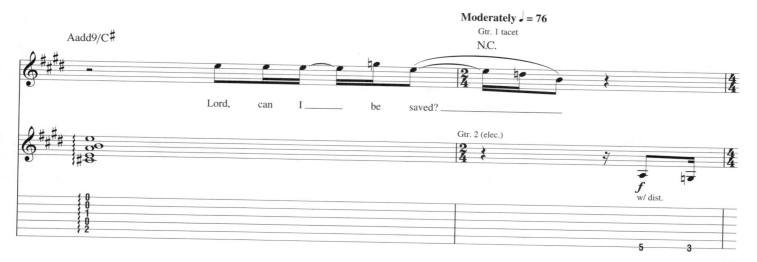

Lord, can I ___ be saved? ___

Moderately ♩ = 76

Gtr. 1 tacet

N.C.

Gtr. 2 (elec.)

f

w/ dist.

2nd time, Gtr. 2: w/ Fill 1
3rd time, Gtr. 2: w/ Fill 2

wa - ter's so ___ un - kind.
took a - way my ___ world.
drown in my ___ own tears.

Brought me to ___ my knees ___ as I
All they found was a let - ter.
Down by ___ the riv - er, I

To Coda ⊕

drowned in the pour - ing rain. ___
nev - er let ___ her go.
see my life ___ in flames. ___

Down by ___ the riv - er, ___ hon - ey,
The riv - er's our own wit - ness,
Down by ___ the riv - er, ___ hon - ey,

I still ___ see ___ your face. ___
the on - ly one ___ who knows. ___

Oh. ___

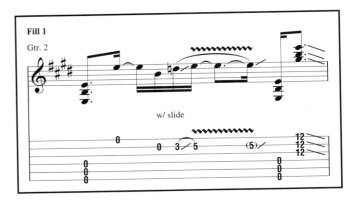

Fill 1
Gtr. 2

w/ slide

Fill 2
Gtr. 2

w/ slide

I call out ___ your name. ___

Lead vocal ad lib (next 7 meas.)

Yeah. ___

SO IT'S LIKE THAT

Words by
Michael Himelstein

Music by
Joe Bonamassa

Tune down 1/2 step:
(low to high) E♭-A♭-D♭-G♭-B♭-E♭

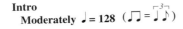

*Chord symbols reflect implied harmony.

Verse

1. Well, I was un-der the im-pres-sion that ev-'ry-thing was __ cool.
train that's run-ning and I'm tied to the __ tracks.

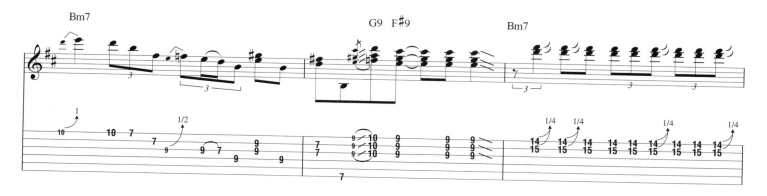

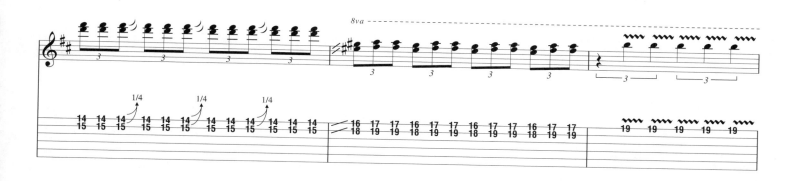

109

WOKE UP DREAMING

Words and Music by
Joe Bonamassa and Will Jennings

Tune down 1 step:
(low to high) D-G-C-F-A-D

Intro
Fast ♩ = 160

Verse

Oh, _____ yeah. _____

Ah. _____

Mm. _____

Guitar Notation Legend

Guitar music can be notated three different ways: on a *musical staff*, in *tablature*, and in *rhythm slashes*.

RHYTHM SLASHES are written above the staff. Strum chords in the rhythm indicated. Use the chord diagrams found at the top of the first page of the transcription for the appropriate chord voicings. Round noteheads indicate single notes.

THE MUSICAL STAFF shows pitches and rhythms and is divided by bar lines into measures. Pitches are named after the first seven letters of the alphabet.

TABLATURE graphically represents the guitar fingerboard. Each horizontal line represents a string, and each number represents a fret.

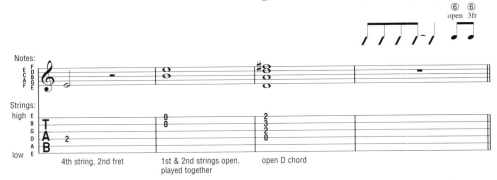

4th string, 2nd fret   1st & 2nd strings open, played together   open D chord

HALF-STEP BEND: Strike the note and bend up 1/2 step.

WHOLE-STEP BEND: Strike the note and bend up one step.

GRACE NOTE BEND: Strike the note and immediately bend up as indicated.

SLIGHT (MICROTONE) BEND: Strike the note and bend up 1/4 step.

BEND AND RELEASE: Strike the note and bend up as indicated, then release back to the original note. Only the first note is struck.

PRE-BEND: Bend the note as indicated, then strike it.

VIBRATO: The string is vibrated by rapidly bending and releasing the note with the fretting hand.

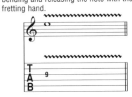

WIDE VIBRATO: The pitch is varied to a greater degree by vibrating with the fretting hand.

HAMMER-ON: Strike the first (lower) note with one finger, then sound the higher note (on the same string) with another finger by fretting it without picking.

PULL-OFF: Place both fingers on the notes to be sounded. Strike the first note and without picking, pull the finger off to sound the second (lower) note.

LEGATO SLIDE: Strike the first note and then slide the same fret-hand finger up or down to the second note. The second note is not struck.

SHIFT SLIDE: Same as legato slide, except the second note is struck.

TRILL: Very rapidly alternate between the notes indicated by continuously hammering on and pulling off.

TAPPING: Hammer ("tap") the fret indicated with the pick-hand index or middle finger and pull off to the note fretted by the fret hand.

NATURAL HARMONIC: Strike the note while the fret-hand lightly touches the string directly over the fret indicated.

PINCH HARMONIC: The note is fretted normally and a harmonic is produced by adding the edge of the thumb or the tip of the index finger of the pick hand to the normal pick attack.

PICK SCRAPE: The edge of the pick is rubbed down (or up) the string, producing a scratchy sound.

MUFFLED STRINGS: A percussive sound is produced by laying the fret hand across the string(s) without depressing, and striking them with the pick hand.

PALM MUTING: The note is partially muted by the pick hand lightly touching the string(s) just before the bridge.

RAKE: Drag the pick across the strings indicated with a single motion.

TREMOLO PICKING: The note is picked as rapidly and continuously as possible.

VIBRATO BAR DIVE AND RETURN: The pitch of the note or chord is dropped a specified number of steps (in rhythm), then returned to the original pitch.

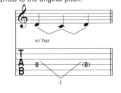

VIBRATO BAR SCOOP: Depress the bar just before striking the note, then quickly release the bar.

VIBRATO BAR DIP: Strike the note and then immediately drop a specified number of steps, then release back to the original pitch.